VOODOO LIBRETTO

New & Selected Poems

Tim Seibles

ALSO BY TIM SEIBLES

Body Moves

Hurdy-Gurdy

Hammerlock

Buffalo Head Solos

Fast Animal

One Turn Around The Sun

Kerosene (chapbook)

Ten Miles An Hour (chapbook)

Body Moves

Unabashedly sexy, lush with music, joy, and longing, Seibles' voice sings an inverted lullaby, rocking the cradle, but waking us Up! Up! Up!

—Naomi Shihab Nye

Hurdy-Gurdy

Listening to Tim Seibles sing the poems in this sizzling collection is like listening to the voice of the griot praising, admonishing, cursing, blessing, and calling us together. ... As a reader of poetry, I appreciated his exquisite crafting and cool, streetwise lyricism. And as a somewhat envious fellow poet, I wish that every rich, textured stanza were mine.

—Patricia Smith

From the "sweet scat" and "jump rope hymns" of wonder and wistfulness to the transformational, lithe, sexually charged energy of jazz, *Hurdy-Gurdy* earnestly explores the differences between what we want, what we get, and what we must be willing to pursue at any cost. This is an exciting book— at once fluid, shapely, and steady as stone—whose tensions lead us to an authentic meditative wholeness.

—Mark Cox

Hammerlock

Tim Seibles' versions of our changing and growing American speech range widely, from anguish to comedy, from transcendence to earthly bewilderment. The joy of reading these poems is like overhearing a very smart, crazy neighbor's thoughts as they move between philosophical inquiry and praise for the everyday.

—Li-Young Lee

Tim Seibles will get you in his hammerlock and won't let you go till he has taken you into the center of American politics and pop culture, the minds of birds, the Tao te Ching, your body, your so-called clor, your so-called race. He lights up everything like the candle at the heart of the lantern. A houseful of voices speaks through him in language so tenable, you'll at times feel bruised, at times made love to. I read a lot of poetry. I've never read poetry like this.

—Reginald McKnight

Fast Animal

One could say that Tim Seibles' sixth volume, *Fast Animal*, is a collection of poems that aims to map the coordinates of maturity...but Seibles is not content to wax philosophically about roads not taken; rather, he opts to enmesh us in experience—both lived and imagined. These poems instruct us that wisdom is most available to us in those moments when we are apt to lose our way. Ranging across the urban thoughtscape, Seibles' poems insist that signposts are all around us; here in the form of a comic book hero's solemn purpose, there in the memory of a first crush. With poems whose ambling cadences and formal edginess situate the heartrending infatuations of adolescence alongside the shuddering deliberations of middle age, Seibles engenders the lyricism and phrasing to be found in the most affecting rhythm and blues, insisting that it is only by transgressing borders (of ignorance, fear, shortsightedness) that we can discover a universe full of wonder and grace.

—Herman Beavers

In *Fast Animal*, Tim Seibles has reached a new level of sophistication and emotional depth. His tone has nuances that are so subtly and seamlessly woven together that laughter and sorrow are often present in the same poem. Built like one single sustained song, this book is alive with music, ardor, and wit that flow in utterances that are uniquely his and his alone. But in *Fast Animal* there is also a new urgency and tender wisdom that speak to—and about—"the great storm/ each man each/ woman walks/ as if beneath/ a second sky."

—Laure-Anne Bosselaar,
The Hour Between Dog and Wolf and *A New Hunger*

Fast Animal is a collection of poems that reminds us, with every powerful breath, of our common humanity. Tim Seibles is a poet of extraordinary sensitivity. His images are luminous—almost unbearably vivid—evocations of the world around us, past and present. These are narratives of hard-earned wisdom, exhilarating discovery, sly humor, and defiant subversion, from recollections of first loves to the desire to punch a certain former president. Few poets can write about a kiss with such delicate precision, or capture with such immediacy the fear and courage of an African-American man "sitting in a park/ in Virginia holding a white woman's hand." Seibles is, above all, a praise-poet. The "Ode to My Hands" is a particularly joyous celebration, reminiscent and worthy of Neruda. May there be odes to Tim Seibles. May there be praise for Tim Seibles. May we all learn from this poet what he didn't know, and then knew.

—Martín Espada

[Seibles] writes with a lucidity of heart and head and soul about all subjects he gets his hands on. His poems are vivid and succinct and have an ease and a grace and wholeness about them.

—Amy Gerstler, Editor of *Best American Poetry*

One Turn Around the Sun

Through precise language, striking and intimate images, a paradox of smart irony and disarming sincerity, and a persistent awareness of the pressure of economic and political realities, Seibles offers us a rich and memorable inquiry into a life. When I turned the last page of *One Turn Around the Sun*, I felt like I'd just finished a wonderful novel.

—Ellen Bass

About trying to understand his parents, Tim Seibles says, "It's like watching them through thick glass," but the distortions of magnification and detailed focus that mark these poems, which are as much an homage to family as they are a confrontation with the complex feelings that surround the fact of aging, represent an opportunity for Seibles to write some of his most affecting, clear-sighted poems to date. These are profoundly vulnerable poems that are distinguished by the risk and daring that we expect from our best poets. Those of us who have come to enjoy Seibles' lively language code-switching, his alertness to the political and social realities of our time, his alluring sensuality, and his splendid and welcoming humor will be wholly satisfied by this beautiful collection; but his careful charting of a poet's life beginning with the accident of his birth, the elusive story of his parents' histories, as seen from this present personal and historical moment, make this one of his more important collections to date. Seibles is an essential American poet, and he wears this mantle with sheer mastery, endearing self-deprecation, and grace in *One Turn Around the Sun*.

—Kwame Dawes, *City of Bones: A Testament*

Tim Seibles. When the world grows nostalgic, he swings real. When the world turns bitter, he stretches out his arms in verse. When the world tries to deny, he stares it in the face and tells the truth. Then asks it for a dance. I'm tempted to say *One Turn Around the Sun* is Tim Seibles' best book, but that'd be like saying Beethoven stopped at eight symphonies.

—Cornelius Eady, *Hardheaded Weather*

VOODOO LIBRETTO

New & Selected Poems

Tim Seibles

etruscan press

Etruscan Press
Wilkes University
84 West South Street
Wilkes-Barre, PA 18766
(570) 408-4546

 Wilkes
University

www.etruscanpress.org

Published 2021 by Etruscan Press
Printed in the United States of America
Cover painting: *Contemplation*, 2017 © Solomon Isekeije
Cover design by Lisa Reynolds
Interior design and typesetting by Julianne Popovec
The text of this book is set in Adobe Jenson.

First Edition

22 23 24 25 5 4 3 2

Library of Congress Cataloguing-in-Publication Data

Names: Seibles, Tim, author.
Title: Voodoo libretto : new & selected poems / Tim Seibles.
Description: Wilkes Barre, PA : Etruscan Press, 2021. | Summary: "In a language that is
both frank and emotionally charged, this book wrestles with issues of family, race, religion,
sexuality, and more generally, the journey from innocence to hard-hearted experience.
The poems, at times, disagree with one another in terms of tone and perspective, but this
further clarifies the complexity of coming to grips with all that's inscribed in the American
story. To grow up in a particular neighborhood, city, or country is to be all but blind to the
many defining characteristics of the place, which seem natural as the sky. This collection
chronicles the intimate and intricate twists and turns of a person-a black man in this
case-discovering himself while simultaneously coming to a complex and unflinching un-
derstanding of the world into which he was born. It is the imaginative agility of the figures
who inhabit this work that fuels its revelations"
-- Provided by publisher.
Identifiers: LCCN 2021004657 | ISBN 9781733674188 (paperback ; acid-free
  paper)
Subjects: LCGFT: Poetry.
Classification: LCC PS3569.E475 V66 2021 | DDC 813/.6--dc23
LC record available at https://lccn.loc.gov/2021004657

Please turn to the back of this book for a list of the sustaining funders of Etruscan Press.

This book is printed on recycled, acid-free paper.

for James Marshall Hendrix, my spirit guide all these years

for the beloved, Jennifer Natalie Fish

for The Stairwell Crew, Brotherhood of Hearts & Words

and in remembrance of my parents:

Thomas Sumner Seibles III & Barbara Bluford Seibles
1928–2019   1927–2020

ACKNOWLEDGMENTS

I would like to thank the following publications, in which several of the new poems have appeared:

A Gathering of the Tribes: "Game Day," "Sometimes Freddy Blues Villanelle"

Beloit Poetry Journal: "Amusement Park," "It Had Been a Long Time"

Little Patuxent Review: "Come Home, Lady"

The Dalhousie Review: "The Dead Play Blues Villanelle"

The James Dickey Review: "Praise The Lord!" "The Dollars"

The New Guard: "Seeking Asylum"

The Southampton Review: "Extra Bright Blues Villanelle"

And we must constantly encourage ourselves and each other to attempt the heretical actions our dreams imply and some of our old ideas disparage. In the forefront of our move toward change, there is only poetry to hint at possibility made real. Our poems formulate the implications of ourselves, what we feel within and dare...

—Audre Lorde

And I go on believing in the possibility of love. I am convinced that there will be mutual understanding among human beings, achieved in spite of all the suffering, the blood, the broken glass.

—Pablo Neruda

The essence of oligarchical rule is not father-to-son inheritance, but the persistence of a certain worldview and a certain way of life imposed by the dead upon the living.

—George Orwell

Poetry is rebellion. The poet was not offended when he was called subversive. Life transcends all structures, and there are new rules of conduct for the soul. The seed sprouts anywhere...we wait for enormous changes every day; we live through the mutation of human order avidly: spring is rebellious.

—Pablo Neruda

CONTENTS

OPEN LETTER II

Seventeen years ago, as a preface to my fourth book, *Buffalo Head Solos*, I wrote an "Open Letter" in which I tried to develop some ideas about poetry—what it could mean, what it might *do* given the "American predicament." I spent a good bit of that letter discussing boldness and daring, "stomping in with bad breath and plaid boots," which struck me as necessary if poetry was going to become a more muscular presence in the cultural fray, especially where younger minds are concerned. I still think poetry could use more *attitude*: an infusion of *kick-ass* punctuated by a guffaw. The Spoken Word scene embodied some of that, yet many so-called "page poets" resented the dramatic aspects of spoken word and doubled down on the majesty of the page. This blinded them to the song, the rambunctious energy, the *duende* that was to be found in the best "stage poets." To hell with decorum. The daily world still bleeds under the governance of bad ideas—*technophilia*, Pollyanna visions of the *free market*, the fetishization of war, "old time religions"—and the resulting cynicism that greenlights those who would destroy the Earth. The unruly, more beautiful, most subversive, and sweetest things have, somehow, got to get said.

I've heard people talk about "inappropriate" poems, as if good poems should be comfortable on a leash, shouldn't howl too loud, wag too hard, or bare their teeth. Beyond the dog metaphor, I believe poems must do a share of the work that can't be done without risking offense. Not to say that poems *should* offend, but that poems can't be afraid to tussle if saying the essential thing runs the words out of bounds, burns some bridges, headbutts a few deacons. Why did I fall in love with poetry in the first place? Because I found new rules in residence there, new ways of renegotiating my life that existed beyond official approval. I'm not only talking about the range of plaintive song but the reach of the ecstatic too. Poems can certainly give us names for what grinds our guts, but they can also widen the embrace, remind us of our right to cultivate and savor all that's marvelous—which includes the fact of our own presence in this world!

Going through the last forty years of my work, it became clear that my life in poetry has always been driven by the belief that poems could escort both unshackled imagination and political daring into *any* community. This still strikes me as a fundamental good if we cherish the possibility of *liberating* social transformation, not just for people of color and other marginalized folks but for everyone who has suffered the many entrenched constraints on thought and witnessed chronic injustice wearing the face of the norm.

As a newly minted senior citizen, I can better see my own sharpening madness as it has taken shape variously over the four decades I've spent trying to build a home in poetry. I don't mean a *career*, but a place where I might be understood in ways that are simply unavailable in the daily shellacking of self I perform to approximate a character that can keep a job and pass for normal. I know I'm not alone in this daily self-erasure, this constant striving for the palatable face. We become so adept at *adjusting* that maybe we never fully comprehend how many masks we're obliged to wear.

Take *manliness*, for example: How do dreams of invulnerability distort a man's sense of reality and possible action? How many times have I worn the cool face, taken the tough pose to hold my place among men? You have to wonder what this requirement is doing to us. I think of all the young brothers who've joined a gang, in part, to prove their *hardness*—which leads them where? There must be an analogous performance of femininity that confounds young women as they begin to entertain the possible arc of their lives. At what point does the premium placed on prettiness and softness compromise their investment in physical strength and intellectual ferocity?

It's also worth considering this in the context of racialism. The *double-consciousness* that Dubois described as a prominent feature of black life has innumerable tangents, none of them helpful. And, more than this, how exhausting is the prevailing assumption that black folks are here mainly to bear witness to our troubles? We are here—like all people—to delight in our lives: to make whatever noise, dance whatever dance best marks our time on Earth. Rage and grief will be paid their due, but love and play and ravishing wonder are equally a part of our story.

For me, poetry is the place where—if I am not intimidated—I can say the most dangerous, most tender, most mysterious things I know, where I may find the same in the work of other poets. It is a place where *clarity* subverts the half-said, the never said, so that wakefulness might be magnified, emboldened. Such crucial speech sustains my hunger to see more than *the way it is*—more than the way it's been. I'm talking about *pure voice*, the untamed voice, the voice with no rider, no bit in its mouth. Inasmuch as any utterance can be a sign of what *is*, a poem may contain those moments where head and heart make a jailbreak from all that under-imagines what we can know, what we might become. The future is fundamentally an unfolding of how we conceive of ourselves right now.

Of course, we think and write in a socio-political context. Even the language we speak bears the lush abundance and *blind spotting* of myriad generations, but writing a poem is a chance to rub the language against the unique thing inside a person and maybe bring about a sound, a vision that could not be born without the singularly distinct self. In the hands of Jimi Hendrix, for example, the guitar *spoke* in ways never imagined—because of what he heard *in his own head*. Had he allowed the great wall of precedence and expectation to corner him, he would not have conjured the sublime *telling* that unleashed an entirely new vocabulary. Similarly, Cecil Taylor with the piano. Likewise, when we read/hear pure voice: a Lucille Clifton, a Vasco Popa, a Primus St. John, we must reconsider what *consciousness* is. Are we awake? What exactly have we done with this life? I find myself disgusted with the polite prattle of my well-managed, *workable* mind. Perhaps part of what compels someone to spend a life in poetry is the chance to hear the secret arias of the authentic self, that nearly wild thing—too amazed, too appalled to be afraid.

I'm not talking about navel-gazing, the kind of introspection that embraces the clever gobbledygook of self-congratulatory *see-into-me* babble. I'm talking about the ways in which we might address the shared world. If someone can say *the realest shit*, those sounds, those silences, those jagged breaths will carry some of the flavor, some of the storm that allows us to recognize—in the words of a stranger—versions of our own craziness, our own chronic anxieties. Though poetry is often overlooked as a critical element in society, *this* is one way that a sense of community is constructed and sustained. Being enabled to see ourselves in the lives of others, we will find it much harder to do harm, much more difficult to underplay the suffering of anyone. When William Stafford wrote "I am the one to hum until the world can sing," I think he meant to remind us of poetry's power to affirm, in the same instant, the life of both writer and reader.

I cannot imagine my life without Pablo Neruda or June Jordan solely because they have written so much of what I wish I could have said. Though neither knew of me nor had any explicable way to engage my particular sensorium, each gave me the gift of feeling known, *spoken for* in all my oddness. And what about the many sensations for which we, as of yet, have no word, no exact noise—those emotions that float in the space between those we can name—or those that are, somehow, a composite of conflicting feelings? Isn't this the rightful territory of Art—of *poetry?* However deliriously I have written over these forty years, however far I have fallen short of the essential utterance, I have tried to be faithful to the pursuit of that mean-what-you-mean, lovingly mad, *ain't-this-how-it-be-sometimes?* song.

I was a teenager during the late '60s, which might account for my faith in art as a way to widen the boulevard we walk with our restless hearts. My adolescence was deeply affected by The Last Poets, Mahalia Jackson, Les McCann—and the speeches of Dr. King and Malcolm X. Though we find ourselves in a period of similar social upheaval with people "takin' it to the streets" while defenders of the status quo omit facts and otherwise distort history, this moment in 2020 feels unlike that earlier moment. Undoubtedly, today's social media has intensified the pixilation of culture. You can go online and find those *who only say what you already know*, which could be the death knell to complex civil discourse, of which literature—on and off the page—*is* a significant part.

The last four years have been a warning, a reminder of this nation's not-so-distant past: the willful stupidity, the legislated cruelty, the ruthless hunger for wealth that has engraved the terrible inequities we still must endure. What can poetry *mean*, what can poetry *do* in a country where tweets and re-tweets of demented rhetoric can move millions to "follow" into a dim-witted and venomous alternative reality? I believe poetry can support and sometimes spearhead the resistance to bigotry and related *dumbfuckery*. I believe a poem can help us see—in both intricate and intimate terms—our shared vulnerability. At the very least, such understanding is the beginning of sanity, which must be the bedrock of any chance we have to make a world where "good sense and good magic" hold sway.

—Tim Seibles
November 25, 2020

from *BODY MOVES* (1988)

What does what it should do needs nothing more.
The body moves, though slowly, toward desire.
We come to something without knowing why.

—Theodore Roethke

BIG MOUTH

A few nights ago
you slept
with your mouth open
and the moon
slipped inside

because you have
such a big mouth
and now
your eyes glow
like a jack-o'-lanterns.
Now

every evening
when you look out
the sparrows rally
and the plants lean
toward you
as though sensing
another dawn.

Don't try
to explain. Imagine
even tonight, the trillion eyes
left heavy
and moonless. Don't
look at me. You slept
with your big mouth
open
thinking you had
every right
and the moon
snuck inside.

Already
the broken sky
has started chewing on stars
and soon the night
will be dressed
like a widow.

Don't say anything. Don't
apologize. Don't
think of all the lovers
by an otherwise moonlit lake
fondling each other
clumsily in the blackness
getting nowhere
because of you
and your
big mouth.

Be glad
that your head glows. Be glad
that you'll never
need a flashlight
if your car dies
on a country road.
You slept
with your mouth
open, open

like the bell of a tuba
only bigger   much
bigger   and the moon
just couldn't
resist. So be happy
for that
inner light. Be happy
and shut up   shut up
shut up.

A MOMENT

It's Sunday afternoon
and Monday already seems
unavoidable.
Your eyes drift
like withered gulls
looking for a place to land
just for a moment
a moment as long and perfect
as the legs of a dancer.

When you lean back
your brain slides
to the back of your skull
like a baby pig
in a bowl of mud.
You're almost gone.
You want to tell the world
to kiss your ass,

but all over the house
a phone keeps ringing—
room after room, you grog around
picking up each receiver,
saying hello, sounding polite.
The voice at the other end says
Hey, what's all this about
telephones? Lie down.
Get some sleep. You stagger
to the next phone. Sleep
rides your back like a huge
retarded bear whose fur
and damp, friendly breath
smell like the quiet shade
of an old cedar in the undiscovered
middle of a forest

where you'd love to lie down
and whisper to the buttercups—
just for a moment,
a moment as long and perfect
as the legs of a cheetah
upon whose back
you would ride from the city,
through the country,
beyond this Monday

into the heart of sleep.

THE LEAP

It's morning. Your mind leaps
like a man with his ass
on fire. You're
late for work. It is
your ass. The boss is already
polishing the paddle. You hate

the pitying eyes of others
watching you approach his door.
You ask yourself *Will God
be like this*—big bloodshot eyes,
orthopedic shoes, blockhead
bowed and slowly shaking
as though you were simply
some sad bastard come too late
to repent. You open The Door.

It is God, but She's beautiful
and relaxed, wearing a tight
black dress, sipping
Manischewitz. There are
your good friends. There are
your parents. There's *Perrier*
on ice. God smiles and opens
Her arms. You're stunned. You
point to yourself. A music
falls over you like a fleece.

You're holding God's hand and
touching God's hair. Her arm encircles
your waist and suddenly you taste
the holy lips—you smack yourself
and straighten up, but God says
"Don't be shy" and fingers your ear.

You don't know what to do.
Your father grins, "That's God, son.
It's alright." You feel so good
so many places with such
little effort—and to think
you were an agnostic.

After finding such a buddy
you will never work again
and you will not pretend
you're Moses.
You will simply live
as though your brain
were made of a hundred
drunken fish. It's morning.

It will always be morning.

WHO KNOWS

There is a self in the middle of yourself
That knows that it knows that it knows it knows

What more can be said   what else can be told
There is a self in the middle of yourself
That knows that it knows that it knows it knows

How much of you is dead   How much has been sold
There is a place in the middle of the middle
That knows that it knows that it knows what goes

Who burned your bread and broke your fiddle
There is an eye between the eyes
That knows that it knows but it never shows

Who owns the world and gives you little
There is a weed in the middle of yourself
That knows that it knows that it knows it grows

Which root runs too deep   What sleep eats your nose
There is a stream way down in the valley
That knows that it knows that it knows it flows

Who sails your ship while you work the galley
There is a wind in the middle of yourself
That knows that it knows that it knows it blows

How much of you is covered   How much is unclothed
There is a moon in the blackest black night
That knows that it knows that it knows it glows

There is a self underneath yourself
That knows   that it knows   *that it knows*

DOUBLE DUTCH

In the afternoon tiny stars of sweat
beam from my skin, a mockingbird
nabs a bug, the seedy head of a dandelion
goes bald in wind, and I'm starting
to remember an ice cream cone
I got one summer. I was up to my waist
in weeds. There were the weird berry trees,
the red apartments, and me
with a bucket full of grasshoppers.

In the alley down the hill three chocolate girls
two turning two ropes swaying 3-6-9,
the goose drank wine, the monkey chew tabacca
on the streetcar line and the one in the middle
jumping double dutch as though there were
no time and no other way. Later

I was going to the schoolyard. I was going
to play football with Melvin, Snooper,
and Jimmy-White. They would be waiting
in the big shade by the monkey bars, and maybe
Crystal and Vanessa still in T-shirts
with their "big stuff." Me and the fellas
would make desperate plans for the night—
I knew what Mel would say. I knew we itched
for those soft shapes under cotton. Then
my mother called me. She was across the street
holding an ice cream cone.

It was lemon.

THE WORD 1964–1981

In Philadelphia
I went back to the school
we integrated. The bunch of us
had no idea how big a deal it was—
our parents behind us saying
Be good now. Stay outta trouble.
But we were fourth-graders
and the teachers didn't want us.
What could we do? I became
the class clown. Clyde grew the brain,
and Reggie wore fake ties all year round.

Meanwhile, "For Sale" signs
sprang up like tombstones.
The cautious parents
were getting their young lilies
to the suburbs. There's not a
white face anywhere in the area now
except the principal who
drives into the city at dawn
to lord over his black castle—
but the field is still there,
and the bright yellow bases and
the twelve-foot fence I smashed into
leaping for a football. On some
of the side doors you can
still find the word *Nigger*.

THE SNAIL

Sisters,
I am weak of your kisses
the wanting of them
the scheming for them, even now
with the sun out, even now
as I say it, even now
while the world warms in the sky's wide mouth
I am broken
for the lack of kisses. I am bereaved
of all the tongues shut away
in the black moonlessness behind teeth
behind smiles behind faces bruised
with unspent desire—what are we doing
so far apart? How many times has evening come in
like a woman and found me
kissless as a snail? How many hours
have I bullied the silence
talking about lips about the way a good kiss
spills into every untouched crevice
of the brain, talking
till my own ears bled of the words
and the sun rose again only to find me:
the same mad snail, talking
through the frost on my window
to the nubby grass, to the squirrels,
the paper boy, to all of America, talking
about the wasted night and the nights
that will be wasted
while I'm drowning in the kisses
the way everyone is drowning
in that hot river of kisses,
never tasted never tried.

THE KISS

José, do you remember the first kiss
you did with your mouth open?
But of course not, since you are
such a Godzilla, you will spend your life
waiting like a man whose bus never comes.
Anyway, when I was fifteen, there was this girl
named Jane. Because of her, most of us
walked around with something like a rock
in our pants—and the neighborhood was struck
by an epidemic of wet dreams. Sometimes
they were hand-assisted but still
it was Jane's fault: she always looked
like she needed to be kissed, not savagely
but hard enough to require Vaseline on the lips.

It was a bad time for me and my friends
at this small Lutheran school. There
were few girls and fewer still black girls.
In the public schools, rumors of *fast pannies*
ran shining like sunlit satin down the halls—
stories of big-legged babes who would take on
maybe five lucky dudes at once!
At our scrawny little goodie-goodie school
we were enslaved by the prospect of a kiss,
even a little smooch not held for an instant.
A hug would've been a big deal.

Anyway, because Jane was so fine, I figured
trying for her would be useless—my hair
wouldn't grow and afros were big back then.
Back then, if you were dying in the street
without a big bush, most girls would just
leave you for the buzzards   and the guys
who talked to Jane had afros so big
they looked like walking trees.

But by some sweet scratch of luck, Jane
mistook my hopelessness for poise
and hinted that I should call her sometime.
Of course, I tried to be cool but, José,
it was all I could do to keep my heart
from ripping my shirt. That night,
my nervous words scrambling over the phone,
I arranged to visit her. On Friday
with the moon out and a big mouse
in my gut, I walked the eight blocks
to Ellum Street—mouth dry,
pulse stuttering, but every strand
of my measly hair oiled and perfect.

When she opened the door, she looked
so good I had to squint or my eyes
would have wrestled her to the floor.
There was music and just enough light
and water, which I needed badly.
If the time came I didn't want her to
think my tongue was a dust ball
and pull away disgusted. We sat
on the couch listening to *The Delfonics*,
their voices spinning silk into the air.
My left hand crept

onto her shoulder. My breathing stopped.
I had to make a real move or be a chump
forever: I leaned over. I kissed her cheek.
I waited to be crushed like the desperate
roach I was, but she said nothing and
the slow music kept spilling over us.
Then, possessed by some perverse ghost,
I dove into her ear. José, I am surprised
that her head isn't flooded to this day—
that ear! My tongue tracing
the crescent curve and down to the bit
of wax inside, the top of my brain
singed with the taste of it.

I could still be there now

if she hadn't led my lips to hers
and pulled me down into the wet,
warm wilderness of her mouth:
a tiny jungle, my brother, but one
from which I am still climbing out.

LOOKING

Brothers,
I am sick of burning
for women, sick of saying
Look at her! Look at her!
Lord, have mercy. I am sick of this
ticklish ache, these body whispers, this pubic smoke
that creeps through my veins till my brain
is choking, sick the way a dog must
get sick of summer: tongue touching
the street, tail dragging, his balls
full of June. I am sick of wanting
the big legs of black women, of watching
them pass with those high, holy
half-moons of ass swimming side
to side like round, finless fish.

I am sick of tight pants—
the way they ask to be pulled down the way
an orange begs to be peeled. I am sick of all forms
of bralessness, especially when the blouse is thin
and the nipples keep trying to peep through
like eyes fighting a blindfold, like delicate,
bite-sized bulls charging gently through
a matador's cape. Of course, I am sick
of slit skirts and stockings: downtown
the women walking and with each step a flash
of thigh—a sly whisper of what sings
a little higher, the muffled chorus of lingerie
living in that eternal twilight above the knees
beneath dresses behind smiles. I am sick

of bearing this broken halo, sick of being
blown this way and that by the beautiful winds of women—
and the dancers too, even with their strong legs, their
rippling backs, their suggestive agility—I want

none of it. Not the velvet dark of a señorita's eyes either,
nor the silk forest of her hair, not even her tongue
made smooth and delicious by the constant rolling of r's.

Brothers, tell me nothing of the blue eyes, the curls,
the ebony skin, the flowering of ankle into calf,
of waistline sloping into hips. Say nothing of the
snugness of snug shorts and nothing of sweet, full lips
whose sexual wings beat the mind's thin air
until even the soul kneels and weeps. Don't
mention the possible paradise and all the paradise
lost because I'm drowning in this deep river
of women. My lungs are filled with looking—
I am sick, sad and sorry I ever listened
when puberty called.

WHAT HOLDS YOU

There are places in your body
that no music can possess. This
is not a good night for dancing.

Outside the wind pulls a wet comb
through some trees and mistletoe
spiders in the bare branches.

You feel an obsession coming on—
someone you can't do without.
Ever since sundown Thursday

something has been turning
in your belly like a gear in a watch.
You can't help but imagine

the moon-glazed skin
inside her blouse and the invisible
rising of her breasts as she breathes.

Tell yourself *It's just a mood, it's*
only evening—it's January.
The temperature has been strange,

but what holds you, what really
keeps you talking to yourself
is that smile, the lush pink

of her lips and her mouth,
which must taste like rain.
This is your brain's favorite

weather—a possible lover:
her hands the color of candlelight
opening toward you—the night

gathering your heart
in its heavy vines. If she
came to see you, if she wore

a silk jacket and nothing
but the breeze underneath
what clock could strike that hour?

It's late. You should
sleep. You have already
called twice. New words

from new alphabets
are taking over
your life.

WHO

for the Lewitzky Dance Company

Who doesn't
want to dance
to be inside the body
not somewhere beside it
to feel the arms and legs
hot and clean in a clear lake of air
like fins, as though every limb
were a fish, for a moment
free of the water, out of the world—
the body, strange as a planet
reeling in its own soft sparkle

Who doesn't want to dance
to let the body go
gracefully mad, to fall
into the music as though
from a cliff—every muscle a feather
every three feathers, a bird—every bird
bald, blind, and falling
as though the fall itself
were the dance, as if the music
were a wind holding you up,
as though in motion the body
is a leaf is a new fabric
better than feathers better than water

Who doesn't want to remember
the feet, to wash them in music
to feel gravity's tireless kiss
bringing you back, pulling you in
as if there were only you and the Earth
and music were the sea
and the body were a small ship
with lungs as its sails—as though

breathing were dancing and dancing
were living and living
were enough. Who
doesn't want to dance?

NOTHING BUT FOOTBALL

for Melvin Strand

I

Brother, those days in the schoolyard
playing football with the sun
preaching heat to the asphalt, when
we thought everywhere was Sharpnack Street—
those were good days: you and me
and all the moves we used, our feet
fast and smart as God, our heads saved
from everything but dreams
of getting the ball and that single
glorious, ever-present possibility of *touchdown*.

II

Our sneaks laced with NFL Highlights—
Mel, with a football in our hands we were
right as priests: celibate, heaven clearly in sight,
ready to abandon the world just to get closer
just to fake the hell out of anyone
trying to stop us. They couldn't stop us:
you stutter-dipped, I snake-slipped, anything
to spin-shimmy away clean as light, slick as sweat,
holy thieves in a forest of moving trees. What
hymn, what hidden but unquestionable singing
did we dance to then?

III

I hated to play against you, trying to read
the mystical sermons of your feet, the blur
of your *Converse* sneaks, that sudden

cut that always came sure as dark,
and the finishing gallop that left us
praying to your back. There was nothing
more beautiful, no creature more purely
one with its escape, and I have loved nothing
and no one more than that twelfth summer
when we roamed the schoolyard beyond
our parents, riding a football into this life:
every day a new game. Every catch a blessing.
Every opening, a parting of the sea.

HOPE

Listen. Someone is dead.
The eyelids drop like two leaves
into the shallows of a pond. Listen.

The phone rings. A low voice
bleeds through the wire: the bad news
crowds everyone toward that one

last breath. Listen. We are
still breathing. All over the world the lips
keep shaping the words. Listen.

We are not dying—
the brain stays in its private room
spreading the map like a Caesar.

New cells chirp like toads
in the body's shallows. Listen.
It is *this life* that matters.

THIRD WISH

for W.H. Auden

Sometimes some things are just hard to know
So often I think there's so much I've missed
But someday today will be long ago

I watch women walking, I watch children grow
This looking sends me such a fragile bliss
Sometimes some things are just hard to know

Down here, the days fall like toy men in a row
I pay all my bills—I check off the list
But someday today will be long ago

I keep asking questions, but the questions don't know
When you whisper a prayer, does it land like a kiss?
Sometimes some things are just hard to know

I keep a straight face—I look calm even though
My parents never told me it would get like this
But someday today will be long ago

If I knew it I'd know it   and I'd let it show
I walk through the world like each step's my third wish
Sometimes some things are just hard to know
But someday today will be long ago

THE DRAGON

for Carlo Pezzimenti

José, I wasn't always bald.
It took many thousand beers
to make this belly
and many thousand kisses
to chafe these lips. Maybe
I'm not so fast anymore and one
gentle woman can tire me out
for a week, but I'm smiling
and the ladies can walk past
fanning the air as if to fly
with their fabulous hips
and I don't need to douse my head
in the creek. My brother, it is no sin

to be content, to love what lives
inside our faces that makes the birds flee
and the strays come shyly to us.
But it can never be that I'm
only pleased—terrible things
will happen to us! Look at the cricket
hung in the web and the spider
in the beak of the cardinal—
the bloody streets, the broken faces
and the soldiers who keep tonguing
their rifles. These are the teeth

of the dragon whose jagged breaths
tear through us like blades.
How much killing can a man see
before he dies from watching?
How much of what is big inside us
is dead from trying to come out?
But, José, it's alright: we are not
so easily beaten. There is the music

of guitar and your mad black face
to live for.

When we talk like this
with the night balding with the sun coming
with the everything breathing fire on us
I want to tell you that this *is* Eden.
No one was cast out. The world
has always harassed us. If it isn't love
it's *milk and shit in the brain.*
If it isn't the morning come too soon
it's the night setting in like a stain.
The insects, the germs, our jobs
eating us intently and this hard season
of aging separately no matter how we try
to hold on—and you, José, if you are not
enraged by the lack of kisses you are
snorting like a two-legged bull at America.

But there is less to it than this.
There is the cracked joy of being mortal
and knowing it, the knowing that
even as you set fire to yourself
and come flying out, someday
you will get a rest
that no one can interrupt.
So dream all you want of an island
or some kiss   or worry yourself
with missiles and white presidents.
The quiet will come just the same.

I know you think I'm a soft,
happy-eyed old dog curling up
with these days because
I'm afraid to fight, but sticking out
your mouth will do nothing now.
We are no longer children, my brother.
We must perfect our illusions.

from *HURDY-GURDY* (1992)

Nothing perishes, it is merely lost till a surgeon's electrode starts the music of an old player piano whose scrolls are dust. Or you yourself do it, tossing in the restless nights, or even in the day on a strange street when a hurdy-gurdy plays. Nothing is lost, but it can never be again as it was. You will only find the bits and cry out because they were yourself.

—Loren Eiseley

TRYING FOR FIRE

Right now, even if a muscular woman wanted
to teach me the power of her skin
I'd probably just stand here with my hands
jammed in my pockets. Tonight
I'm feeling weak as water, watching the wind
bandage the moon. That's how it is tonight:
sky like tar, thin gauzy clouds,
a couple lame stars. A car rips by—
the driver's cigarette pinwheels past
the dog I saw hit this afternoon.
One second he was trotting along
with his wet nose tasting the air,
next thing I know he's off the curb,
a car swerves and bam! For an instant
he didn't seem to understand
he was dying—he lifted his head
as if he might still reach the dark green trash bags
half-open on the other side of the street.

I wish someone could tell me
how to live in the city. My friends
just shake their heads and shrug.
I can't go to church—I'm embarrassed
by things preachers say we should believe.
I would talk to my wife, but she's worried
about the house. Whenever she listens
she hears the shingles giving in
to the rain. If I read the paper
I start believing some stranger
has got my name in his pocket—
on a matchbook next to his knife.

When I was twelve, I'd take out the trash:
the garage would open like some ogre's cave
while just above my head the Monday Night Movie

stepped out of the television and my parents
leaned back in their chairs. I can still hear
my father's voice coming through the floor:
"Boy, make sure you don't make a mess down there!"
I remember the red-brick caterpillar of row houses
on Belfield Avenue and, not much higher than the rooftops,
the moon, soft and pale as a nun's thigh.

I had a plan back then—my feet were made
for football: each toe had the heart
of a different animal, so I ran
ten ways at once. I knew I'd play pro
and live with my best friend and
when Vanessa let us pull up her sweater,
those deep brown, balloony mounds made me believe
in a world where eventually you could touch
whatever you didn't understand.

If I was afraid of anything, it was
my bedroom when my parents made me
turn out the light: that knocking noise
that kept coming from the walls,
the shadow shapes by the bookshelf—
the feeling that something was always there
just waiting for me to close my eyes.
But only sleep would get me, and
I'd wake up running for my bike, my life
jingling like a little bell in the breeze.
I understood so little that I
understood it all, and I still know
what it meant to be one of the boys
who had never kissed a girl.

I never did play pro football,
never got to do my mad-horse,
mountain goat, happy-wolf dance
for the blaring fans in the Astrodome,
never snagged a one-hander over the middle

against Green Bay or made my snaky way
down the sideline for the game-breaking six.

And now, the city is crouched like a mugger
behind me—right outside, in the alley behind my door,
a man stabbed this guy for his wallet, and sometimes
I see this four-year-old with his face all bruised,
his father holding his hand like a vice.
When I turn on the radio, the music
is just like the news. So what should I do—
close my eyes and hope whatever's out there
will just let me sleep? I won't sleep tonight.
I'll stay near my TV and watch the police
get everybody.

Across the street a woman is letting
her phone ring. I see her in the kitchen
stirring something on the stove. Farther off
a small dog chips the quiet with his bark.
Above me the moon looks like a nickel
in a murky little creek. This
is the same moon that saw me twelve,
without a single bill to pay, zinging
soup can tops into the dark—I called them
flying saucers. This is the same
white light that touched dinosaurs, that
found the first people trying for fire.

It must have been very good, that moment
when wood smoke turned to flickering,
when they believed night was broken
once and for all. I wonder what almost-words
were spoken. I wonder how long
before that first flame went out.

THE MOTION

Ah, but the spirit moves in physical ways—
the wind swims a field, a teenage girl grins
slow and sly, and what steady ruckus does the blood make
running the body's blind streets.

The afternoon is a big house sprung with minutes.
Light chimes on a woman's bright brown hair.
Her strong calves whisper; my heart sings
like a bruise. Luck spins like a June bug crazed

by what glad music?—it must be the sky bringing
sky, it must be a tribe of ants whistling
at a crumb. Everything makes a noise,
every crooning wants an ear—everywhere I go

a woman is dressed in her own shining.
A cat lands, a little boy traps his shadow
against a fence, and the eye pins all this
with one fast hand! How can the world

be in the world? My skin grown loose
as a brood of birds—I could fly
out of myself: naked, the soul would be
less than a word, a web of air

a grabbing   without fingers
but the spirit moves in physical ways
and with it rises this righteous fever.

This slight tickling, this light madness—
it's just the dust of a day blown dim.
Night swings its tail.

FOR BROTHERS EVERYWHERE

for Jas Mardis

There is a schoolyard that runs
from here to the dark's fence
where *brothers keep goin to the hoop, keep*
risin up with baske'balls ripe as pumpkins
risin toward rims hung like piñatas, pinned
like thunderclouds to the sky's wide chest
an' everybody is spinnin an' bankin
off the glass, finger-rollin off the glass
with the same soft touch
you'd give the head of a child—

a chile with a big-ass pumpkin head,
who stands in the schoolyard lit
by brothers—postin up, givin-goin
takin the lane, flashin off the pivot,
dealin behind the back, between
the legs, cockin the rock an' glidin
like mad hawks—swoopin black with arms
for wings, palmin the sun, throwin it down

and even with the day gone, without even
a crumb of light from the city, *brothers*
keep runnin-gunnin, fallin away takin
fallaway Js from the corner, their bodies
like muscular saxophones *body-boppin*
better than jazz, beyond summer, beyond
weather, beyond everything that moves—

an' with one shake they're pullin-up
from the perimeter, shakin-bakin,
brothers be sweet pullin-up
from the edge a' the world, hangin like
air itself hangs in the air,
an gravidy gotta giv'em up: the ball

burning like a fruit with a soul
in their velvet hands, while the wrists
whisper backspin, and the fingers
comb the rock once—givin it up,
lettin it go, lettin it go like good news
'cause the hoop is a well,
a well with no bottom, *an' they're*
fillin that sucker up!

MEEP

I used to root for the rabbit
in his sneaky quest for that fruity cereal—
"Raspberry-red, lemon-yellow, orange-orange"—
and I hated those big-headed little brats,
especially the boy when he'd say,
"Silly rabbit, *Trix* are for kids!"
I always wished he'd smile, *OK, one bowl*
won't hurt, because it really wouldn't have.
I used to console myself believing
the silly rabbit swiped a bunch
between commercials.

And I used to cross my fingers
for the Coyote too: sometimes, running
like a maniac, his legs bulging
from ACME muscle builder, he'd get so close
I could feel the Roadrunner's tail feathers
tickling his nose, but suddenly "Meep-Meep!"
And the road was smoke all the way
to the horizon. The Coyote seemed
ruined, the way he'd knot his brow
while his pointed face fell slack.
I would shake my head and wonder
if he ever got to eat anything *ever*—
and why didn't he give up on that bird
or occasionally go for something slow?

Being six or seven, I guess I understood
the difference between cartoons and my life,
though I admit I couldn't figure out
why they never talked about going
to the bathroom—even the wise Mr. Peabody
must've wet a tree sometime   and Sherman
was a little boy like me.

It's amazing the way I believed so well
in the world: that basically
it was a place to live happily
ever after, that the only hard part
was waiting to get old enough
to stay up late and go outside
whenever you wanted. I don't know

about the world anymore. It doesn't
look like anybody actually gets
what they want. But last Saturday
I was watching cartoons with my niece
and when the Coyote started gaining
on that fast-ass little bird, I leaned
forward in my seat just enough
to catch myself feeling hopeful.

YOU DAMN RIGHT

So much light
from one star and tree shadows
painted on the backs
of squirrels and one grackle throwing
his meanest voice: an evil one-
man band with whistles, broken
cymbals and a snuffly
nose, marching up and back, scolding
the grass and anyone who passes,
his blue-black stark
as a bad mood on a beautiful day—
like the day he tapped he
chiseled his way out of that
bitter egg to find the sky
a new color too far away

and his mother stuffing who-
knows-what into his mouth, into
his mouth, into his mouth and what
was she always squawking about—
about how careful he needed to be
about the world being impossible
to believe; then the sudden *So long,*
good luck!—that bird's foot
in the butt, him scrambling
for his wings, the green
earth jumping up with all its
jagged teeth, his shoulders
burning as he tried the steep
ladder of air, feathers like fingers
clawing at what appeared to be
nothing at all, like the light
filling his eyes, and him:
blacker than any five
good nights sewn together.
How could he have known

what would be required? How
could he know what a
cat was, what a gun was, what
a man was—and lightning and
heartburn and hard-falling
sleet? And time
slipping past like a friend
who owes you money, like
a burglar with all your
brand new stuff   and how did he
fit into the scheme anyway—
and if he really didn't
*What in the hell
was he doing?* Of course
he's pissed off and *you
damn right* he gonna cop
an attitude and nobody
better say shit about it
neither.

ONE

Dishes in the sink

Outside, the sky: a fat man in gray—
a big bag of rain on his back

Thoughts in my head like a
family of rats

Like centipedes under a rock

Late June and light smeared
on this page

The lamp never forgets
what to do

Last night I dreamed
someone

was biting me on the face

Voices from the alley: two boys
with pellet guns trying

to kill something—

Look   Look   There's one

AFTER ALL

Let's say you're black and you walk in
this restaurant and as you take your seat
you notice you're the only one there
darker than blue: the waiters and waitresses,
the hostess and customers, even the cooks—
all of them could walk into a snowy field
and vanish, but you think *No big deal, it's*
cool, no need to go Frederick Douglass on'em.

But soon the peekaboo sets in: you look up
from buttering a roll and notice a middle-aged
mother combing your face like a gutsy,
low-flying pilot on reconnaissance and
another lady with a stack of grayish-gold,
highlit hair begins snapping her glance
at you and away, at you and away,
as if some kind of suggestive cucumber
were slowly emerging from your forehead.
Then one old, bald, Burl Ives looking guy
just stares at you with something between
a grimace and a grin stuck on his face.
Yeah, and you know he'd love to break
into a little *Jimmy Crack Corn and I Don't Care*
with his fat little lobster-colored neck extending
and retracting, his thumbs pinned under his arms,
elbows flapping, knees wobbling—Goddammit!

Now you start to feel weird; you check
your fork for evidence that someone
sneezed on it. Don't get a kink in the gut,
you say to yourself, closing your eyes
for a moment. After all, what's with all this
paranoia? "Kareem Abdul-Jabbarrr!"
the waiter grins, refilling your water. "You
look a lot like him." And you can't remember

anybody black ever telling you that.
You imagine this guy trying to fall asleep
counting black men who fly above
some bright parquet floor: dunking, dunking,
and dunking. You begin to wonder
why your food is taking so long. You recall
stories of the *New* South—brothers testing
the waters of once segregated diners
and getting served entrees garnished with
garbage and spit. After all, there's nothing
that suggests these people marched
on Washington. There are no former Freedom
Riders among these porcelain-colored characters
who blink and nod at each other, carving their meat
into some kind of code. After all, who was
throwing rocks at the people who made
the Selma trek with King?—somebody
was shouting *Niggers go home!* and feeling
pretty good about it. And maybe here they are:
a bunch of *somebodies* out for dinner,
and here you are: crashing the party—
a coffee stain on the lapel of white, white
tuxedo, a kinky hair floating in a glass
of milk   and here comes your food, your waiter
carrying it high above his head. "Ka-reem,"
he says, "sorry it took so long, Kareem—
bet you can't wait."

SHAPE

for the ANC

The P.A. tells someone to
pick up a telephone and I
almost do because in an airport
you can be everybody
but today

I am the assassin
looking for the President
of South Africa. My hat shadows
my face like a sneer.
I have

a blowgun
made from the hollow body
of a *Bic* and one dart
tipped with the piss
of an angel
so angry that even God
sits down when she dances.

The brothers see me
and nod, not blinking.
The black women whisper
promises of big-legged nights,
slyly proffering plum-colored lips
between which their smiles
splash like tambourines.

His flight is unloading at gate six—
his escorts mutter Afrikaans
between constipated grins
and glances. Then,
like a cavity

in a tooth, he appears.
He is thinking
about his wife's white
neck in the windswept nights
of Pretoria. In the bathroom
his men check each stall.
His right hand lands
on his zipper. Outside
jets rip into the sky.

When the door marked MEN opens
I am kissing
the silver curl rising
from the fountain. He
pats his hands
on his coat. I lift the pen,
palming it
so only the tip shows—
my first knuckle under my nose,
I could be covering a cough
or yawning

as a tangle of workmen, kids,
parents, and priests
scuffle by. Half-steady,
half-afraid, like a snake-charmer
watching his first cobra
climb into the air, I blow:

one little boy
thinks he sees a bee—a woman
with ragged red hair nearly
catches death in her mouth—the
shoeshine man says something
skimmed his cheek
while the President

takes two short steps and leans
into history. The bodyguards
wheel, hearts wagging
in their throats, guns
glistening in the airport jumble,
but I'm already

everyone else,
already another shape
in a crowd
waiting to fly.

NATASHA IN A MELLOW MOOD

apologies to Bullwinkle & Rocky

Boris, dahlink, look
at my legs, long
as a lonely evening in Leningrad,
how they open the air
when I walk, the way moonlight
opens the dark. Boris, my hair
is so black with espionage,
so cool and quiet with all those secrets
so well kept—those secret plans
you've nearly kissed
into my ears. Who gives a proletarian
damn about Bullwinkle and that
flying squirrel and that idiot
who draws us? America
is a virgin, the cartoonist
who leaves me
less than a Barbie doll
under this dress, who draws me
with no smell—*he* is a virgin.
The children who watch us
every Saturday mornink
are virgins. Boris, my sweet
waterbug, I don't want
to be a virgin
anymore. Look
into my eyes, heavy
with the absence of laughter
and the presence of vodka. Listen
to my Russian lips muss up
these blonde syllables of English:

I wantchu. Last night
I dreamed you spelled your
code name on my shoulder

with the waxed sprigs of your
moustache. I had just come
out of the bath. My skin
was still damp, my hair
poured like ink as I pulled
the comb through it. Then
I heard you whisper, felt you take
my hand—Oh Boris, Boris
Badenov, I want your mischief
riddled eyes to invent
my whole body, all the silken
slopes of flesh forgotten
by the blind cartoonist. I want
to be scribbled all over you
in shapes no pencil
would dare. Dahlink, why
don't we take off
that funny little hat. Though
you are hardly tall
as my thighs, I want your pointy
shoes beside my bed, your
coat flung and fallen
like a double agent
on my floor.

APPETITE

I have eaten the donuts, the plain cake,
healthy whole wheat donuts. I have
eaten them quickly the way the highway
chews the round licorice of Firestone tires.
I have savored the caky flavor with a
born-again gleam in my smile, with my heart
turned wild as a one-eyed pirate
with treasure on his breath. I have eaten
my way southerly and northerly and side
to side, tasting donuts from every angle—
the way a blind man might try the legs
of certain women, women in blue-jean skirts
unbuttoned to mid-thigh, proud women
who stroll the blue boulevards of summer
wearing a thin glaze of sweat
like a damp halo on their labia.

I have eaten the *Fig Newtons* too:
all night without stopping, all night
the way witches roll moonlight like taffy
on their tongues. I did it in the kitchen.
I did it on the lawn. I did it
as though my soul were just a jaw
chewing my life into new hungers.
I attacked without reason like
a great black shark finning
the crowded streets of America—
my nappy dorsal splitting the air,
the pale victims going down fast
like *Fig Newtons* into a man mad
for that squishy feel, that soft
cookie flavor.

And the pretzels,
those laced boomerangs of twisted bread

through which a dark finger might drift
like a thunderhead through the sky's
sheer blouse. I have eaten them all
except for one, crouched like a felon
behind that bag of barbecue chips,
but he is mine. I will eat him
as surely as Europe ate South America—
just knock on his door tomorrow;
no one will answer.

And I regret nothing and I am
not sorry and I don't feel bad about
wanting so much of what I like: some days
I sit all afternoon leering
at a box of gingersnaps. Other times,
without warning, I am biting big chunks
out of something—just like *Flo-Jo*
yums up the meters with her big stride.
With my hands and eyes, I am riding
teeth-first across this life, as if my
appetite were the only way out of this
lonely skin I'm stuck inside,
but it's late: night nibbles the city—
all the avenues cool wantonly
like cakes.

THE BALLAD OF SADIE LABABE

for Carolyn

Sadie LaBabe   was a magic sister
Lord, even a blind man   couldn'a missed'er
Her sultry skin   was dark as shade
Her mind cut sharp as a butcher's blade
And the brothers who stared   at Sadie's thighs
Would shake their heads and moan and cry

'Cause Sadie moved like water poured
The shapes she shaped had angels floored
She knew her walk turned wind to fire
A wink from Sadie turned brains to mire

The mellow fellas tried to talk that sly
They'd high-sing, "Sadie!" when she walked by
But if she stopped   to pass some time
Their lines went stale   and sank to slime
She yawned, she'd heard it all before—
Stuff bad boys write on bathroom doors

'Cause Sadie pours like rivers move
Her black skin rocks men toward the blues
She won't be mine, she won't be yours
She bit Eve's apple down to the core

Now, JT Kade   was Billy-Dee handsome
His humble home they called *Love Mansion*
He was ice cream cool   and built like a panther
Whatever the question, JT was the answer
The sistas crowned him King of The Land
He could make a girl faint just by holding her hand

So one fast day this last July
King Cool JT came boppin by
Now Kade had come   from way up in Philly

His eyes were steady, his lines were chilly
He said he'd come down Dallas way
for this heavy hittin hammer they called LaBabe

'Cause Sadie loved like honey tasted
She'd groove you till your life was wasted
Her tongue was silk, her touch was satin
She'd soothe you till your hills would flatten

But Sadie heard what the sistas said
About this brotha who broke their bread
She made the pledge: "This Saturday night
I'll be home alone by candlelight
And if this Kade   is whatch'all say
I won't mind much if he comes my way

'Cause Sadie's heart   could hold an ocean
She moved more ways than there was motion
Light tight be phat   and tall be low
You gonna maybe-with-Sadie, she gonna stop your show

Three days went past and kept on goin
By Saturday night a light breeze was blowin
With candle shine flecked in her eyes
Sadie sat lazy while the crickets cried
Her blouse was cotton, her shorts were suede
She had big doubts about this Kade

But from the porch there tapped a noise
And through the screen she caught his voice
"Say, Lady Sadie, won'tcha let me in
I got some wine and some time to spend
I'm knockin here   'cause I know you're there
Wanna slide my hands through your thick black hair"

So Sadie smiled   and licked her lips
Said "Greaze and slide under since your so slick
The pleasure's my treasure, we don't need no wine

I like your style and I've heard you're fine—
Let the body be danced and the soul be dazzled
Let's make love shapes till the stars get frazzled"

They talked awhile   then he touched her face
She twined her arm   around his waist
The chatting stopped   the kissing started
The routes they used had not been charted
They rocked the sofa   then bumped the door
They bruised the stairs   they warped the floor
The storm they raised   blew out the candles
He held her hips like they had handles
A whole day passed   and neither seemed tired
If sex is electric   this couple was wired

So Sunday went off when Monday morning came on
Sadie stood up and stretched, but Kade was gone
The grapevine says he's in a home
For those who run where none should roam
They say he sings, he stutters, he raves
About some lady he calls LaBabe
For him the world has come unhinged—
He yells "Sadie loves like a big fish swims"
The doctors scratch their heads and frown
They drug his milk   to calm him down

While Sadie sips soda by a swimmin pool
Her mind is clear, her skin is cool
Sometimes she feels a little sadness
For drivin Kade to that sweet madness
But Sadie holds what most let fall—
If you gonna half-step   don't step at all!

'Cause Sadie played   in the Garden of Eden
She tamed the snake   and taught him readin
She won't be mine, she won't be yours
She ate Eve's apple   and asked for more

ALMOST

No wind   Whole days go by
and I don't remember

Under the tree pile the acorns
and their brown caps

Where is it now

I mark down what words I can
Sunlight soft enough

to sit like a peach
on my shoulder   Sometimes

I almost see how it was

And faces of people I've loved
appear where just before
I saw glass scattered in the street

Where is it now

When I was a boy
I would blow on my hand
and watch very closely

to see if I could see the air

SLOW DANCE

for Savannah

Some days I can go nearly an hour
without thinking of the taste
of your mouth. Right now, I'm at school
watching teenagers fidget through a test.
Outside, the sky is smoky and streets are wet
and two grackles step lightly through yellow grass.

Two weeks ago, in Atlantic City,
I stood on the boardwalk
and looked out across the water—
the railing was cool, broken shells
dappled the beach—I had been
playing the slot machines
and lost all but a dollar.
I tried to picture you in Paris,
learning the sound of your new country
where, at that moment, it was already night.

I thought maybe you'd be out
walking with the streetlights
glossing your lips, with your eyes
deep as this field of water.
Maybe someone else was looking at you
as you paused under the awning
of a bakery where the smell
of newly risen bread buttered the air.

I remember those suede boots
you wore to the party last December,
your clipped hair, your long arms
like the necks of swans. I remember
how seeing the shape of your mouth
that first time, I kept staring
until my blood turned to rain.

Missing someone is like hearing
a name sung quietly from somewhere
behind you. Even after you know
no one is there, you keep looking back
until on a silver afternoon like this
you find yourself breathing just enough
to make a small dent in the air.

Just now, a student, an ivory-colored girl
whose nose crinkles when she laughs,
asked me if she could "go the bathroom,"
and suddenly I knew I was old enough
to never ask that question again.

When I look back across my life
I always see the schoolyard—
monkey bars, gray asphalt, and one huge tree—
where I played the summer days into rags.
I didn't love anybody yet, except maybe
my parents, who I loved mainly when they

left me alone. I used to have wet dreams
about a girl named Diane. She was a little
older than me. I wanted to kiss her
so bad   that just walking past her house
I would trip over nothing but the chance
that she'd be on the porch. Sometimes
she'd wear these cut-off jeans and a scar
shaped like an acorn shone above her knee.
In some dreams I would barely
touch it, then explode. Once

in real life, at a party on Sharpnack Street
I asked her to dance a slow one with me.
The Originals were singing *I'll never*
hear the bells and, scared nearly blind,
I pulled her into the sleepy rhythm

where my body tried to explain.
But half a minute into the song
she broke my nervous grip and walked away—
she could tell I didn't know
what to do with my feet. I wonder
where she is now   and all those people
who saw me standing there
with the music filling my hands.

Woman, I miss you, and some afternoons
it's alright. I think of that lemon drink
you used to make and the stories
about your grandmother, about the bees
that covered your house in Senegal, the nights
of gunfire, and the massing of frogs
in the rain. I think about the first time
I put my arm around your shoulder. I think
of couscous and white tuna, that one lamp
blinking on and off by itself, and those plums
that would brood for days on the kitchen counter.

I remember holding you against the sink
with the sun soaking the window, the soft call
of your hips, and the intricate flickers
of thought chiming your eyes. Your mouth
like a Saturday. I remember
your long thighs, how they
opened on the sofa, and the pulse
of your cry when you came and
sometimes I miss you
the way someone drowning
remembers the air.

I think about these students
in class this afternoon, itching
through this hour, their bodies new
to puberty, their brains streaked

with grammar—probably none of them
in love, how they listen to my voice
and believe my steady adult face,
how they wish the school day
would hurry past so they could start
spending their free time again, how
none of them really understands
what the clock is always teaching
about the way things disappear.

LIKE THIS

All afternoon someone watches
the shadow of a branch
climb the legs of a chair,
and from someplace behind her
you can hear the scratchy whine
of a radio not quite tuned, but *climb*
is not the word; the shadow
moves like something poured, spilling
up rather than down
the wooden legs—and
though she is not
thinking exactly this,
the woman knows that climb
is not the word—she is not
climbing out of this mood;
in fact, she is falling—

just as she fell awake
this morning—the alarm
tripping her up
into the world, the sudden
buzz like a catapult, and now
from this altitude her bed
is a blurry speck, hard
even to remember: blue
sheets? Was the pillow
soft? Her whole apartment
a tiny rectangular box
somewhere down there
where once she had crossed
and uncrossed her legs,
and the woman thinks that
if she really were high up
like a jet, like someone standing
no-hands on the wing, she

would not be so concerned
with the inch by inch
of a shadow taking over
a chair; she would be
climbing hand over fist
through the air, using her
thick, nappy hair as a
rudder, thinking *why*
haven't I always lived
like this?—while all the radios
in America whimper
the simulcast news
of her defection
flying and filling her
blouse the way a swimmer's hand
silvers with ocean, her
strong arms turning
the beige shore
to smoke as she weaves
the far water
into a second skin, a shadow
she can leave there
like something spilled
across the floor, something
like that one   there
that one, behind you
climbing.

POEM

In a hundred years   I will have
forgotten this night   this
whir of traffic from the avenue

I will have forgotten
this voice   this short bridge
of words   this light scratching
at the door

Let me go down to the river
where the water is clear
I am tired of the city

In a hundred years
maybe less   I will have forgotten
the iridescent shine in the eyes
of the living   and the mind's black fire

and this windy October this
quick turning of leaves
will be a single speck of dust
in a grave   nobody visits

Friends   what rainy blues
is this   with such slow wailing
coming from my wrists

Where did I get this stack of Mondays

I throw up my hands   and my hands
do not come back to me   not
in a hundred years either
I have already forgotten
why I needed them

just as I can no longer
remember those nine months
inside my mother   and that early
perfection   of understanding
nothing in the world

SOON

for Carlo Pezzimenti

Not even in the grave will it be this quiet

the smell of sunlight   the sparkle of children
the folding of air as someone walks through it

I listen but I don't hear anything
like this noise trapped inside my teeth

I want to say that soon someday
we'll all be underground

and the earth will not be warm

I think right now we should hold on
to each other   and tell the stories
till our hearts melt like mints in our mouths

but here come the happy shoppers with their silver crosses
their TV-hugging eyes their heads stuffed with fish

Sometimes I can hear the blood
singing in my arms

and there is no sound for the dead

Like right now with the sun broken and the slow
colors of dusk long shadows in your eyes

you can almost remember what you
were thinking   what it was that
as a child you knew   that one morning

when the plants let you watch as they began to grow

When I lie down at last   when they finally shut the lid
all I know will be found in the head of a match

I wish I could open the secret right now

that says why we can't keep letting each other die like this

RAIN

Take a glass of water.
Pour it in the street.

After a while   it will
come back to you
from the sky.

It may be many
months   years even

but that
April will come
that one November

with the one
small cloud

looking for you.

And even if it doesn't
even if it never never comes

all those hours
with your thirst

your memory
licking the fire-blue sky

will make your
hard brown face
a leaf

shining
in whatever rain
there is

STORIES

for Reginald McKnight

I'll probably never die.
My life will just go on and on,
on days like this especially.
All of my life will be composed of days
where nobody in my city kisses or makes love,
days where a single black-winged butterfly
bothers a tall blue spruce,
where the air barely brushes the hair
on my wrists, where the sunlight
has nothing to do.

Sometimes I sit outside clipping my nails
and there's a glint of metal from a window
across the street and I think *This is how
it'll end for me.* I'll be fuckin around
with my thumb and some frustrated dentist
with a Winchester will shove me out
of this life the way some dusty kid
brushes a ladybug off his knee. Right
then, I can feel the crosshairs settling
just behind my ear, the bullet clearing
one thin path through the wind: it's
afternoon, the smell of exhaust oils the air.
I see myself tipping over with this funky
river of music inside my head, but I'm
still here—as far back as I can see, there I am
with this gang of hours growing behind me.

When I was about nine,
two teenage guys, Lonnie's brother
and his friend who said he had a knife,
took me to this place near the railroad tracks.
It was summer. My father was at work.
My mom was at the Food Fair steering a cart

that had one of those wobbly back wheels
that got on her nerves. When we reached
the thickest bunch of trees, they stopped
and I thought I was gonna get
stabbed. The friend said, "Drop
your pants," and when my red shorts
hit my sneakers he smiled, "Them too,"
meaning my dingy underwear with the
drunken elastic, and I stood there shrinking
with my T-shirt covering halfway to my knees.

My friends were back in the schoolyard
playing *Dead Block*, sliding jelly-jar tops
across the concrete, trying to get
to the 12th box, trying not to land
on the skull in the middle, probably
not thinking of me at all. I thought
about how I wouldn't want to be found
dead without my pants on, how my parents
would be ashamed. "Lift up the shirt," he said,
and there I was, scared to death,
my thimble-sized jammy bald as a minnow,
while they laughed and pretended they might
take my clothes and tie me to the tracks.

I won't ever die. I'm positive—especially
on days like this when I'm not even sure
if I'm sad or just a little rundown. Especially
when the chinaberry tree keeps letting one
yellow leaf fall and, up on the telephone wire,
a mourning dove coos softly, maybe
for company, maybe to calm itself down.

I admit I wanted my body to be a saxophone—
I thought the air wanted to be music
and I wanted to make love like a sizzling
angel, like some sort of jazz god
whose every note was a glyph

from the alphabet of fire and time
grew up all around me, while I
just talked and wanted.

Once, I got kicked out of World History
for goofing in the back row of class.
Mr. Groobie told me to shut up, so
I stuffed my chest with badass, said,
"What are you gonna do if I don't?"
It felt good to feel the class swell behind me,
to watch the teacher turn red and shrink,
but by the time I got home I just knew
nothing would stop my father.

I went up to my room. It was around 3:30.
My father worked till five. I remember
watching the secondhand glide—the fear
filling me up as if I'd been swallowing
those ragged undershirts my mother used
for dusting. I thought maybe if I was
outside raking when he drove in, things
might go better   or maybe if I was studying
in the living room when he opened the door.
The clock's face seemed almost sorry
when his key cracked the lock. I only
wanted to be dead before my mother
gave him the news, before
I had to straddle that black chair
in the basement, before I saw him
snatch off his belt.

I bet my life will drift on and on
like some kind of blind fish that
can't really figure out where it is—
on days like this especially, especially
with dusk moving over the Earth
like a woman lying down to the noise
of girls chanting jump-rope hymns:

all over lightning bugs and their
tiny lanterns, the blood in my brain
full of phosphorus like bay water.

I envy the dead their worry-free days:
no more roaches roaming the kitchen,
no bigots, nobody smirking at your shoes,
no more waiting for some bonehead
to call you back, nobody wondering if
you're married, no bills, no changing
your mind or needing a shower or wincing
at someone's sultry strut, no music
for setting the mood, no one to meet
for lunch, nobody stealing your wallet, no
reason to be nervous, no more mosquitoes,
no allergies, no Presidents, no nausea,
no bad weather, and no more news
about people dying. But I'd rather be
above ground running the weeks always
coming back to Monday   Mon- -day
like two notes some crazed bird croons
as it circles your life.

Sometimes, with the right morning,
I go out, let the rain spell my body
and I think about the stories, how they
shine inside us, how they must
come together somewhere   and make
no sense at all but rather remind us
that *once upon a time*, we were real,
that all kinds of stuff happened
and the result was our lives:

I was riding the XH bus to Germantown
Lutheran Academy—early spring, I guess—
feeling a little blah because my mom
made me eat *Cream of Wheat* for breakfast
when I just wanted some cinnamon toast.

Then, at Washington Lane, a mob
of Germantown High babes got on.
I was standing by the automatic door
halfway to the back, feeling more and more
like the private school eighth-grader I was
when this really foxy white girl crowds in
sorta beside me, sorta in front of me.

She was wearing red fishnet stockings
and a black miniskirt. Her hair leaned
toward blonde. I was wearing my
GLA blazer and this cornball
silver-green tie. She smelled like
strawberries and cigarettes. At the next stop
another bunch crammed in and
suddenly her right hip was set firmly
against my left. I believed she would
move to make some space
between us, and when she didn't,
something like a flock of winged mice
filled me from belly to throat.

Until then, my only interracial moment
consisted of rubbing Karen Goldsmith's calf
on the pretense of touching the birthmark
behind her knee. So being a weaselly
little horntoad with the vapors of smoke
and fruit hazing my soul, I eased my body
bit by tiny bit leftward, holding my breath
until my jammy replaced my hip
against her—at which point she moved
smooth as a minute hand to the right.

That feeling, that feeling when I knew that
she knew   she had pinned her butt gently
against me—well, I think about it sometimes,
especially on days like this when the sidewalk
is stoked with summer and the ants are running,

when no one in my city can be bothered
with a kiss, especially on days like this when I'm
right in the middle of living forever
and a crowded bus blunders by and I see
the people packed inside pretending they
don't really see each other, pretending
they aren't seriously dying
to taste that strange communion, to feel that
nearly accidental spark pressed into their skin.

from *HAMMERLOCK* (1999)

...I stand up next to a mountain
I chop it down with the edge of my hand
I pick up all the pieces and make an island
Might even raise a little sand

'Cause I'm a voodoo chile...

—Jimi Hendrix

CHECK OUTSIDE

They believe that if they remain
frightened enough for long enough
things won't happen. You know—*things*.

Listen to a city late at night:
the deadbolts clapped into place,
TVs spitting on the floor, upstairs
mothers stammering *Jesus*
into their clasped hands.

But things will happen. Even here
with everybody here. People are going
to do some more things. You see it
all the time. Starting now

and from now on, weather is weather
and news is weather too.
Who do you think is behind
those uniforms? Your plans:

your ideas   about tomorrow.
Even now, the blood burns
in your ear—a story. You want
me to tell you a story.

But right now, we're right
in the middle of something really
funny, and let me tell you, it's
something like a story, all this.

People with chips, heavy chips
on their shoulders. People with a few
tricks up their sleeves.   have
got to do some more.   things.

Check outside—how the wind runs
from some exact somewhere.
That man near the wall
by the 7-Eleven. What's he got
in his hand?

WHAT BUGS BUNNY SAID TO RED RIDING HOOD

Say, good lookin, what brings you out thisaway
amongst the fanged and the fluffy?
Grandma, huh?
Some ol bag too lazy to pick up a pot,
too feeble to flip a flapjack—
and *you* all dolled up like a fire engine
to cruise these woods?

This was your *mother's* idea?
She been livin in a *CrackerJack* box or somethin?
This is a tough neighborhood, mutton chops—
you gotchur badgers, your wild boar, your
hardcore grizzlies   and lately,
this one wolf's been actin pretty big and bad.

I mean, what's up, doc?
Didn' anybody ever tell you it ain't smart
to stick out in wild places?
Friendly? You want friendly
you betta try Detroit. I mean
you're safe wit me, sweetcakes,
but I ain't a meat eater.

You heard about Goldie Locks, didn'cha?
Well, *didn'cha?!* Yeah, well, Little Miss Sunshine—
Little Miss *I'm-so-much-cuter-than-thee*—
got caught on one of her sneaky porridge runs
and the Three Bears weren't in the mood:
so last week the game warden nabs Baby Bear
passin out her fingers to his pals.

That's right. Maybe your motha should
turn off her soaps, take a peek at a newspaper,
turn on some cartoons, for Pete's sake:

this woyld is about teeth, bubble buns—who's bitin
and who's gettin bit. The noyve a'that broad
sendin ya out here lookin like a ripe tomata.
Might as well hang a sign around your neck:
Get over here and bite my legs off!
Cover me wit mustid—call me a hot dawg!

Alright, alright, I'll stop.
Listen, Red, I'd hate for somethin
unpleasant   to find you out here
all alone. Grandma-shmandma—
let'er call *Domino's.* They're paid
to deliver. Besides, toots,
it's already later than you think:
get a load'a that chubby moon up there.

Ya can't count on Casper tonight either.
They ran that potato-head outta town
two months ago—tryin ta make friends
all the time: he makes you sick after a while.

Look, Cinderella, I got some candles and some
cold uncola back at my place—whaddaya say?

Got any artichokies in that basket?

HARDIE

You know how tiny kids walk up to you, raise their arms
and expect to be picked up?—I used to do that: that was me.

Me, with my diaper full and my nose half-crusty.

I remember being eye to eye with the little doors
underneath the kitchen sink—I was a child, seriously.

I used to yank open those cabinets and see the shiny colors:
the orange box of *Tide*, the pink bottle leaking dishwashing liquid
a green *Pine-Sol* thing with big yellow letters.

Of course, I couldn't read, and before I could touch anything
my mom was snatching me back, slapping my hands—

that shit hurt! My hands were really little, really
new like shoots fresh out of the ground:
I was a child—is that clear?

People just put me to bed whenever they felt like it.
People sat me on the potty every other whenever
and said *Go!*

I didn't have any words, just sloppy, muddy kinds of
garbled clucks that tried to be *wordish*—

think of the amount of criticism I got. Criticism
piled on like cold mushroom gravy.

It was like I couldn't do anything right—not a goddam thing!

Picture me in a highchair being pressured to eat.
They might have been dangling a secret agent off a cliff
trying to make him give up something top secret.

I was little. My legs hardly held me up: everybody
stood around poised to catch me—

Ooops!   Ooopsy!   Whoops-a-daisy!

How could I get my confidence?

But now I'm big: I eat ice cream all the time.
I use the *Men's* room—nobody tells me what to do.

Even though I feel like I'm holding onto my life
the way a wounded ant clings to a window screen, I'm

big, big and musty—big enough to hold my baby shoes
in the palm of one hand.

But once I was a kid. I didn't need
deodorants. I sat on my grandmother's lap
and ate candy spearmint leaves.

I wasn't down on white people / I didn't even know
I was black. My whole bag was cartoons—
I was a child, goddammit!

Just a mouthful of Tonka Toys and Lego,
a little guy with no sense of time passing.
Where was everybody going?

Whatever happened to *Johnny Quest?*

Next thing I know, I got this hardie thumping around
on my belly—every morning, fearless,
like my own badass rooster—sunup and
cock-a-doodle-doo!

I couldn't pee with it and nobody would tell me
what it was for.

I wasn't always so worldly, wasn't always a madman
over women's legs either. I spent my first fifteen years
without a real kiss.

I was a child—you think I don't remember?
You think it's easy keeping all this innocence
pent up inside?!

And now, when it comes to money, I'm like some
dizzy insect full of wanting it, like some blind
bluebottle fly tipsy over a mound of shit.

I wasn't always like this.

Parts of me started getting large, growing hair:
my underarms, my crotch, even the tops of my feet.
But I *was* a little boy once—really curious, really
small, really scared.

Is that clear?

COMMERCIAL BREAK: ROADRUNNER, UNEASY

If I didn't know better I'd say
the sun never moved ever,

that somebody just pasted it there
and said to hell with it,

but that's impossible.
After a while you have to give up

those conspiracy theories.
I get the big picture. I mean,

how big can the picture be?
I actually think it's kinda funny—

that damn Coyote always scheming,
always licking his skinny chops

and me, pure speed, the object of all
his hunger, the everything he needs—

talk about impossible, talk about
the grass is always greener...

I *am* the other side of the fence.

You've got to wonder, at least a little,
if this could be a setup

with all the running I do:
the desert, the canyons, the hillsides, the desert.

All this open road   has got to
lead somewhere   else. I mean

that's what freedom's all about, right?
Ending up where you want to be.

I used to think it was funny—*Roadrunner*
the Coyote's after you   Roadrunner

Now, I'm mainly tired. Not that
you'd ever know. I mean

I can still make the horizon
in two shakes of a snake's tongue.

But it never gets easier out here, alone
with Mr. Big Teeth and his ACME supplies:

leg muscle vitamins, tiger traps,
instant tornado seeds.

C'mon! I'm no tiger—
and who's making all this stuff?

I can't help being a little uneasy.
I do one of my tricks:

a rock-scorching razor turn at 600 miles an hour
and he falls off the cliff, the Coyote—

he really falls. I see the small explosion,
his body slamming into dry dirt

so far down in the canyon
the river looks like a crayon doodle.

That has to hurt, right?
Five seconds later, he's just up the highway

hoisting a huge anvil
above a little yellow dish of birdfeed

like I don't see what's goin' on!

You know how sometimes, even though
you're very serious about the things you do,

it seems like, secretly, there's a
big joke being played

and you're a part of what
someone else is laughing at—only

you can't prove it, so you
keep sweating and believing in

your *career*, as if that
makes the difference, as if

playing along isn't really

playing along as long as you're
not sure what sort of fool

you're being turned into—especially
if you're giving it 100 percent.

So, when I see dynamite
tucked under the ACME roadrunner cupcakes,

as long as I don't wonder why my safety
isn't coming first in this situation,

as long as I don't think
me and the Coyote are actually

working for the same people,

as long as I eat and

get away   I'm not really stupid,

right? I'm just fast.

WHAT THE WIND SAYS

after David Swanger

The wind says, "I am the past beside you, a scratch
on your lens, lips that opened easily and wetly,

took you in. You might lose the map, but the road
I poured to your heart will still shimmer. I am

neither air brewing, not either hand set afire, not God
strumming the Earth, nor jeweled anger in rottweiler eyes.

You think you are someone to be reckoned with, a star
pinned above your crotch, your best day
tucked inside your vest like the ace of spades. You

believe what you read is trying to mean something
in some helpful way. Pitiful. Take your thumb
out of your mouth. Mainly, what you miss

matters most—which is why I am the saliva
lost on your neck from a kiss, the slash
in that air where you sit, long fingers slipped

inside you, the shoe dreams cobble while you sleep.
I know you've almost broken through to the present,
only to turn back to a pimple in the mirror.

Since you fumbled at love, you believe the wind
sighs with you   that when you end up
on the wet spot, I know the chill and sympathize.

Forget that shit! Imagine this moment
all your organs humming together like a choir
of roots in damp earth. Is the whole story

wrapped up in *your* destination? Think.

Think of how early becomes evening, how
blind fish find each other from opposite sides
of the dark. Think how sexy I am

because of what I keep from you."

THE APPLE CAKE

for Hermann Michaeli

On days like this,
on Tuesdays, when sad buffalo
moo blues inside me, and what sun there is
fizzles above my crooked hat
like a dud fuse, on Wednesdays
when a man wears his solitude
like an iron yoke, when a woman strings
her necklace with the same rage
that split the moon,
when itchy children lean
against windows, waiting while rain
whips the sidewalks

when all over the everywhere, trouble
chain-smokes and spits, and
people wonder why they
ain't got no money, why the priests
are tipsy with sin, why the police
have turned against them,
on Thursdays, when pigeons
start barking and the rats
have already nibbled God down
to a hairy nose, when every president
is Reagan, when it all seems lost
and wrong and too far
for any luck to reach:

I like to consider your apple cake
smiling on the kitchen counter, dressed
only in its sweetness, its round face
a jubilant island of apple and sugar.
No mere strudel or sloppy cobbler,
it is a baked cathedral of promises
kept—your apple cake opening

like a three-day weekend,
a Good Friday for the mouth, a jailbreak
from the hard, inedible, unbearable city.

How do you do it, my friend?
What is the recipe? More than teaspoons
and cups, sifters and beaters,
the magic must hide in your hands
like invisible fruit: each finger secretly
a buttery bough of apples blazing,
each year of your life changed
to flavor, each memory—even the ones
that bruise soul—a nameless spice,
a lamp intended to glow
in the hope-laden tongue of the world.

The apple cake, a circular avenue
around and around which the friendliest
lovers move—in no hurry
to be anyplace but your arms
forever, for an afternoon—
the sacred window that reveals
the real Earth: a blue ruby
pinned to a golden scarf
of nearby stars, the delicious Earth
done with barracuda greed
and bone-headed hate.

The apple cake itself, a new planet
where everything plays everything and all
is always well: big towns filled
with pals, mambo music, polkas, hip-
hop, the very air tipsy
with baking—where someone lonely,

someone sincerely complicated
can put his arms around
a warm slice or wrestle a big piece

to the floor—and without
saying anything, with only
a parting of his lips,
make a perfect night of it.

Some people were playing cards…and among the players was a young man who at one point, without saying anything, laid down his cards, left the bar, ran across the deck and threw himself into the sea. By the time the boat was stopped…the body couldn't be found.

—Marguerite Duras
from *The Lover*

THIS IS THE REASON

This. This white railing. This
something like sorrow,

something like a scraped knee—
but in your brain. This long wait

with whatever's next
like powdered glass on your tongue. This.

These scratched hands. These dead stars
shuffling the dark. This ache like ice

on a tooth, only
all the time, like a time you

really needed to say something. This
itching scab in your heart.

This something like
not breathing when you're

breathing. This. This
Pepsi jingle, the newspaper,

these insects, this evening, that cigarette.

THE HERD

Some of the light, some of the first light
arrived so softly it could have been dew
drawn from the night air, and in the dim
blue distance thunderheads flickered.

They were still sleeping then, scattered
under trees or in groups in the open,
their slate-colored flanks brightening.

Yesterday, three had been killed, but the wild dogs
were gone now and the scavengers too
and the lake began to show dawn its muddy edges.

What was surprising was that they ever slept
at all with so many things alive in the dark
but they slept well, dreaming exactly what they
dreamed they should dream and when the strongest one
rolled back the silence with a long throbbing yawn,

the others answered, divvying up the air
with staccato croaks, shrill bleats and near-
growls. Some with front legs still bent
beneath them, some with eyes shining
as if they had never before seen the world.

No one knew how long they had been here
or what to call them   or how it was that they began
to understand themselves, what to do, where to go.

But they moved together like a slow wind,
as a wind moves from one place to another
dying off but rising again, the same wind moving.

And when the must broke into their blood
they coupled fiercely, almost in a panic

as if one by one they were beginning to drown—
the heat sliding over each one like the shadow of a cloud.

———————

Once it had cleared the treetops, the sun paved
the veldt bright yellow, and the stilt-legged birds
that had been chitter-whistling since early early
quieted: some stood in the shallows
stabbing the lake for lazy, flat-headed fish.

The herd was eating too, nudging each other for room,
nostrils flexing wet and open. You might have
thought they'd been made for nothing but
filling their mouths, so content did they seem
tugging at the stringy greens with their square teeth.

They were not stupid, though sometimes when weather
changed suddenly, they would simply stampede
barrel-eyed while the rain snapped against their backs.
And if one among them bore some odd marking,
when it reached a certain age, the others
drove it away with headbutts and hard kicks.

I saw it happen once: a female with a bronze color
instead of the usual gray limped a short way
behind the herd, her right foreleg fractured.
Each time she tried to rejoin they attacked—mainly
the bulls and ranking cows—stomping, frothing,
fussing up immense heaves of dust.

The wounded animal appeared confused, not
seeing, unable to see itself, unable to keep
from following, just as the attackers couldn't
stop, couldn't understand what frayed inside
their skulls to turn them against their own.

———————

The dogs were made for this:
their sharp, furry ears barely visible
gliding above the high weeds by the lake
and when they took the open field their feet
kissed the earth for allowing such speed
and the taste of meat and they were upon her
and the air rolled over, so heavy with the smell
of blood, it was nearly animal itself.

Hard to say what went on inside the herd
with death blossoming right there—
or if any had actually watched the kill
or if it made a difference either way.
The dogs would always be there, blind
but for their teeth   and the herd
would continue to find the sunrise
next to the dark, returning from sleep
to offer their young to the flat world.

And was it anything like sorrow
that brought a few back days later
to scuff the ground where that one
with the new face had fallen?

Or just some dumb itch
of memory, some lizard's blink
of déjà vu: the future circling
to take them along.

CULTURE

for Tracy Chapman

Like a wave

When they came they came

like a wave

Not like a wave from the sea
Not like the wave a boat makes cutting water

but like a wave

When they came
they came

and it looked like a big wave
carried them

the way a big wind carries columns of rain

or maybe the wave was them
coming as a wave would come

Not a wave of sorrow
like those that rush the heart
Not a wave of confusion

Not a wave of heat
like one that comes in summer

More like a wave

than a wave

When they
came they came

as you might imagine a wave hurrying
to come ashore

Not like a wave of sound
though they were heard
Not like the wave of a hand
though we did greet them

When they came they just
kept coming

until we couldn't see
across them   until we couldn't
get around them until

looking at them was like looking
at the ocean from an island

and the wave
carried some of us
like a wave

as though in a way we'd
become a part of it
this motion   this constant shove

as though being the wave
meant we couldn't do anything
about the wave

the way water in the surf can't fight
the walking of tides

But this wave
wasn't a wave exactly

but it seemed to seem
like a wave would seem
if one had come

There was something inevitable about it
the way it came as they came

the way it carried some of us along
for a while   for a pretty long while

as though it were our destiny

Not like a wave would
carry something   but like

a wave would carry
something   unlike a wave

like a wave

KEROSENE

after the LA riots, April 1992

In my country   the weather
is not too good   At every bus stop Anger
holds her umbrella folded her
face buckled tight as a boot   Along the avenues

beneath parked cars spent
cartridges glimmer   A man's head
crushed by nightsticks   smoke still
slides from his mouth   Let out wearing

uniforms   hyenas rove in packs
unmuzzled   and brothers strain inside
their brown skins like something wounded
thrown into a lake   Slowly

like blood filling
cracks in the street slowly
the President   arrives   his mouth
slit into his face   Like candles seen

through thick curtains sometimes
at night   the dark citizens
occur to him

like fishing lamps along
the black shore of a lake   like moths
soaked in kerosene   and lit

GOOD HAIR

for Derrick Bell

Like anybody, I would like to live   a long life.
Longevity   has its place.

Much of this is already decided.

But if everybody died tomorrow
what would the point have been?

Power?—the strength to do unto others
and not get done unto?

If I can hit you and not get hit   I can change
your life.

Mmmmm. Nutritious Rodney King.

I lived in the time of the whites.
Europe and America ran the globe.

Like two related sets of big, sharp, smiling teeth.

   "But *my* family never had slaves."

─────────

Let us not seek to satisfy our thirst for freedom
by drinking from the cup of bitterness and hatred.

A lot of this seems settled.
Capitalism makes everything glisten.

   "Come to Jamaica. Come back to the way things used to be."

For who?

I lived in the time of power. Whites?
They had an angle. The had the edge.

They wrote it down. They played it out.

But they left us sports—especially *basketball*.
————

It came as a joyous daybreak   to end the long night
of their captivity.

It seemed like everything we did was a reaction to them.

The music we made, the way we talked.

We started "good hair" and "bad hair." And blues.
And "high-yellow"—and "too dark."

My parents spent their lives proving they were
    "as good as   if not better than."

    "Guess Who's Coming to Dinner?"

I give up. Tell me.

Who *was*   Sidney Poitier   in that movie?

When all of God's children—black men and white men,
Jews and gentiles, Protestants and Catholics—will be able
to join hands and sing in the words of the old Negro spiritual…

What made Sammy Davis   kiss Richard Nixon?
Who made *Stepin Fetchit?*

Power is the capacity to turn people
into money.

In Ethiopia and Guatemala no one
gets rich helping others lose weight.

_____

So History rises up on hind legs and starts
sniffing for something to eat

Something like profit. Something like you. Something
like Michael Jordan. "Be like Mike."

While I lived, I was never exactly sure where I was
bleeding from.

 "Mr. Seibles, where I come from black men   are *black*.
 In Gambia, we would see your light-brown skin, and
 we would not say *brother*."

The marvelous new militancy   which has engulfed the
Negro Community must not lead us to distrust all white people.

And now it is finished. The house no one
meant to build, but

look at it—perfect—even the trim.

_____

Evil has grown so stylish and beautiful.

So young and restless.

 "How come none of the white countries
 get to be part of the Third World?"

Power? How do you ignore power?

I've seen   the Promised Land. I may not get there with you,
but I want you to know tonight, that we, as a people,
will get to the Promised Land!

Sometimes I think my head is going to explode.

Mmmmm. Nutritious Rush Limbaugh.

Imagine someone biting your face over and over,
but you have to keep acting like nothing's wrong.

Imagine someone saying, "But my family
never had slaves."

A lot of days like this.

I lived in the time   when the capacity to kill
and take and feed your fat fuckin face

was power.

––––––––

Times when I think I've just landed from some other world.

Like I don't really speak the language,
but people nod and play along.

What did it mean, does it mean?—being *white*.

I lived in America. It was never quite explained.

NOTE: All italicized passages come from speeches
made by Dr. Martin Luther King, Jr.

NO MONEY DOWN! TAKE IT HOME TODAY—IT'S *YOURS!*

Sun climbs over the trees
and light runs toward you,

runs flailing its fast, golden legs
like a good dog who's been lost for years—

now seen again   *there* in the park
who turns around before you can even whistle

a name, as though just the one wish in your eyes
were loud enough to bring it all back:

the big, shaggy ball of sun blazing like a happy collie
back into your life, licking your face, asking

Where have you *been?*
Where, oh where have you been?

VOCABULARY BROTHER: THE EDITORIAL

after Damon Wayans from In Living Color

Unless I am suddenly uninformed of concurrent hypotheses,
I feel that it is compulsive of me to regurgitate incisively
regarding the matter at hand. In these coitally disruptive times
it often seems that an erect man must step forward and remain
rigid, erstwhile others merely arouse themselves
in the poignancy of their own homes. My primary point
is quite impertinent: however hazardous the recent fellatio
of the community may appear, there can be little doubt
that all of us—black as well as white—wish to be blown
completely out of proportion.

In a parallel manner, I think it must be undermined
that, inasmuch as each man is intangible, his or her
intestinal ambition remains a source of fragrant
advertisement that, in its own way, promotes
the combustion of what can only be regarded
as the inescapable Tampax of modern society—
which is certainly not to plug the seminal point
that in the proper uterus might deserve a wide
speculum of hasty investigations.

Nonetheless, the President's approach to these
vexations could be comparably incentivized to what
heretofore, ipso facto corroborates the untold story
of unanesthetized vasectomy. And finally,
without some dedicated probing into the irrigated
womb of our urban predilections, you and I
could be left in dire need of lubrication, brimming
with future ejaculations in an America frothing
with cultural richness.

THE GUST

for Omar Sosa

In the mind
there comes a moment
when shadows fall back like men
from a gust of something,
when the brain is light
as a fly on your wrist

and in the jeweled eyes of that fly
you see your own six-legged self—
white-shoed, dancing,
swinging on parade—

the gold tuba grown from your lips:
Zoom pahdah cha-cha
Boom pahdah cha-cha
Zoom pahdahhh

HEY

To God's hairy ears, all this sad jibber-
jabber sounds like a bad baby peeing
on a plastic hymnal. Turn out
that serious face. Put down
your poison. In between everything
between us, everything keeps keeping
a cookbook of possible kisses. It is only
by being stupid that we follow
the scared into the lonely.

Listen. Enough money for the church.
Enough dog days. The bank & business boys
cannot stop this mutiny, this late allegiance
to the whispering in the blood. Why
let anybody starve? Why is it
so hard to be happy. *Shhh.*
You already know
what the blood is saying.

Tonight. I am a shadow. With one hand
made of light. This is the beginning
of a new weather—this shared breath, this
open secret. Ghosts of all good kinds
have gathered to shake the *hully gully*
in your thighs. Hey, look how big
the wind is   and still you do not see it.

TEN MILES AN HOUR

The weird thing about the place was the speed of light—
8, 9 miles an hour, tops. *I sweartagod!*
It was beautiful though, the way it felt slowing over you
like a balmy breeze—light slow enough to catch in a,
in a cup, light you could smear on a slice of bread
like jam, light you could rub into your hair like *Sulfur8*.

And there were other things. For example,
just about everybody but little kids could outrun it,
something we never consider here with the photons
clockin 186,000 miles a second. So say you saw
some skinhead muthafucka with a swastika on his cheek.
You could holla, *Hey, you piss-brain, duck-steppin,*
kitter-litter suckin, sick-ass Nazi, then take off.
Once you hit 10 miles an hour you'd disappear
till you broke back to a trot. That's the beauty
of slow light—no muss, no fuss:
now you see a brotha   now you don't.

Anyway, this is how it really went. First,
I should say there were no cars for obvious reasons
and getting to this spot is a long haul on foot:
down this long alley, over three rocky hills,
gotta wade through this one muddy river
and there's a forest somewhere, dark and spooky—
made me feel like Red Riding Hood.
So when I arrive I'm tired and my sneaks are soggy
like I'm wearing wet biscuits on my feet. Everything
looks blurry—like, like when you move a camera
just as you snap the shot.

Pretty soon, I notice nobody's poor   *nobody*—
and I come to this park and there's a sista
straddling this Hawaiian dude on a bench.
Her skirt's hiked up, she got them big legs shinin'

and I mean they're gettin it, gettin it good
to the last drop right there. And it wasn't about
showin off. They coulda been hid way away somewhere,
two good people takin care of business, you know—
T-C'in on the B like it wasn't no helluva big thing.

And there was this bunch of reddish-gold birds,
looked like pigeons—and all these kinky-haired kids
chasing them across the grass with painted leaves
and together they made a noise like someone   someone
munching *Cracker Jacks* near a microphone.
So I just start dancing—no music but that: I just
take off my clothes and start wavin my arms and hoppin.
I'm steady shakin my yams, my jammy's jingle-jumpin,
and pretty soon it's me and two other brothas   then
these Turkish cats fall in on congas   and this
Jewish honey and her extremely fine friend from Laos—
I sweartagod! And then this Ethiopian mamacita, a real
killa-dilla, busts in the circle wit this Mexican
Mississippi-Masala lookin girl, and I turn
to this Eastern Bloc brother named Gustav and holla
*Oh no, say it ain't so—don' NObody need to have
no BODY like that!* So we grab our gear, get dressed
and follow them to this place called Logan's: black tables,
big sofas, soft single chairs covered in lazuli blue.

Somebody hits the dimmers. I ride the light over slow
like, like a loose clump of new weather, and open my mouth
to the first words that gang up inside my teeth. *Excuse me,
ladies, but my blood's all tied in a knot, and I
was wondering if you might help me get it undone.*
Ethiopia nudges Mexico and asks me if the knot in question
might require both of them. *No lie!*
But I don't wanna fade on Gustav; I nod his way. Like smoke
his smile floats over. So she closes her eyes and I see
that her friend's hand has wandered under her dress
lingering there with small, graceful undulations.
I'm diggin it, but I'm not sure what it means. So

I shrug and get ready to step back when Mexico says
Taste this, holding up two wet fingers.

Well, what would you have done? Been scared
and said *Um, no thanks—I'm driving*. Man,
I could spend my life tryin to name that flavor.
Anyway, Alandra (that's her name) gets up wit them legs
that go *all* the way down, and I can feel some story
starting to untell, my body calling *open-says-a-me*
to all its magic doors. Next thing I know
we're dancin to this oldie slow jam:

> *I'm an ever-rolling wheel*
> *without a destination real*

> *I'm an ever-spinning top*
> *going around   till I drop*

You know that moment
when two bodies find out how
they fit together?—as though one torso
is hinged to the other, as though you're both
perfectly matched pieces in some sweet, nobody-ever-
told-you-about-it, sho-nuff forever and always jigsaw?
Me and Alandra are falling into place.

> *You got me going in circles*

Later, we step outside. It's sundown.
You could see the last puddles of sunlight
drying up, going dark, and the streetlamps
slowly throwing their lazy glow like Rapunzel
rolling down her three stories of hair.

I mean—up until just now—I thought I might still have been
standing somewhere in America, but the night held no threat
and across the road, I remember, two men resting in each other's arms.

And her kiss, the taste of her mouth opening like a sleepy carnival

into mine, and Gustav and Genet against the magnolia: fucking
like dancing, like doing some delicious, naked salsa—

my lungs squeezing more and more oxygen into my blood,
my brain bright orange like a tropical fish. Alandra
bringing me into her skin, holding on, taking me up
like some kind of origami bird she could balance on her lips.

And the *not-out* moon, the sharp whelming of what
is never seen   and the voice coming all undone
but for the one long syllable   and *I sweartagod!*

There is a place not all that far from here
where glad drums whistle
all the answers to the riddles of bone.

Say whatchuwanna, but inside my hand
there is a sound, and inside that sound
there is a city, and inside that city
it is early—with you already awake:

your hand like mine, like a rooster
throwing itself open   loud, each finger
a street vendor crowing the first light
free—along with all the big, blue-apple muffins,
the crowded carts of cantaloupe, and the T-shirts

and the clear castle of air,
and everything else   *everything*

from *BUFFALO HEAD SOLOS* (2004)

I believe in the great day
Which will make our paths meet:
I shall wake then from the desert
Seeing you approach with pots filled with water.

—Mazisi Kunene

AMBITION

I.   Cow & Microphone

There's so much I can't
make a sound for: sunrise
on a hillside   or cool dusk
bluing a meadow, late June

or better yet, mid-September
when the first flecks of autumn
begin to walk summer down
from its tall heat.

How can anything living
not love the color light
spends on October—

when the bulls hum
the last unnibbled pasture?
Wonnnderful! Sometimes I think

I could lend my own true music
to that slow farewell: the daylight
bleeding, a whole season turning
away switching its tail   and my voice:

an encyclopedia of lovely noise,
flies open to the first page, and I'm
Ella Fitzgerald's raging treble clef.
I'm a four-legged flugelhorn, a glad

clarinet—the radical ambassador
scatting a voluptuous river of sax,
blowing the rest of the lows
into a dumb herd, while I run the range

of my whole ten-pound heart:

loneliness—the light   always
  a clear view to death   the prevailing
hands of the powerful   and sweet

  sweet grass—the earth's free bread
grown back   and lately, the knowledge
  that an animal like me   can't be heard

exactly—and all this breaks out of my teeth
  into the bovine world. My bruised tongue
at last an angel's lash

  driving the stampede and   shouldn't I
be the Pied Piper? My stomachs are full

  of rare news and the cruel promise
of slaughter. Isn't the other language

  underneath this? Isn't there
one word   that still brands you?

AGO

Awbury Park, June 2002

I don't know where they are now,
Vince and Nahja. Days like these
we'd walk to the park and wrestle
the whole afternoon. Jigsawed
leaves and yellow grass took over
our free nations of black boy hair.

We were twelve—in the ticklish grip
of just about everything. Nahj loved
red shoelace licorice and Vince
blacked big Vs on the backs of his hands.
Trying to pin those guys was like
trying to braid the tongue of a snake
and we laughed the way June sun
beams on trombone brass.

I like to believe the craziness
that made us tackle and roll
blew in from a last storm
of childhood genius, that
blind faith in the glory
of playing whatever you want.
But maybe we had just
found a way to rush the time
it would take to shove past
our parents—a way to wait
without waiting for the years
to let us out:
with no homework, no bedtime
and no reason to clean up our rooms.

This was before we saw
how it was and turned secretly
desperate—before our eyes

were sharpened by sex, before
they killed King   and race
bled all over our lives.

And if Time did anything then,
it only made us younger
or, if it didn't, it only touched us
the way our mothers brushed
our hair—roughly but just meaning
to help us look better.

But it's different now. Nobody
grades my *citizenship*, and my face
won't be smooth again. I can't find
my friends, and when I do, they've strayed
into these half-bald middle-aged men
whose voices I remember *kind of*,
the way I remember the fried apples
my mom used to fix   when I was
still a bacon-headed boy begging
to sizzle along in the world's hot skillet.
But it's different now

and it *ain't the same*: these trees
are bigger than the ones we tussled under
and my tough father has grown
smaller than me and kind, and I don't know
anymore. I don't know what I knew
about not getting pinned to the ground.

But one summer when I was halfway
done with my teens, I heard
my great aunt say she didn't like
"the flavor of thyme," and not knowing
any other way to spell that sound,
I stared at the kitchen wall:

at the flowery face of the plastic clock
and watched the second hand

wheeling its well-worn way around
and I knew, even then, that somehow
without really trying, I'd become older
than those hula-hooping little girls
whirling their skinny hips down the alley

and I was glad to be made
of that many years, but I did
start to wonder

how it would feel and what
on Earth it would mean
when I could actually taste it.

AT 41

Houses   House lights

The river's rippled black sheet

Night

Like twinkle from gone stars
memories can be seen long after

Lives missing lives

I would stand beside my mother at the kitchen window

My brother and my father already across the street

One coffee cup with a red-pink lip print
One box of *Kellogg's Country Corn Flakes*

My big brother and my father going to catch the bus

Memory   like a scratch on the brain
over which the needle skips   and skips

How similar the slight sway of their shoulders

The 9th grader and the biochemist
heading for the S bus

Was there already something the matter then

What's the matter?

How well they did not talk

"Like peas in a pod," my mother said
lighting her smile, hand on my hand

October.   Then.

My bones were still growing
but I couldn't feel it—

any more than I could
understand anything else

I was   actually growing

HARVEST MOON

Big Sister, apple light, kiss
on the river—tonight
make each word a strange dish

each long ache, for once, a gotten wish.
Let this small song brush the big dark back
while you stroll along the sky forever.

Yo, to think such bright shadow, this
black sash, that soft shine She wears
comes spun from a sun flung aloft

the other side of my world. What
cat-eyed glow? What well-keyed
mischief? What

slow hands, deft and delicious, undress
my grim predictions, juice up
my ragtime shoes? It happens

on the now, while the moon is unshy.
My soul—yo, otherwise a pale theory—leaps
into the visible, trying his slippery spin

on the glad lap of Earth. Uncles, mothers,
sly lovers, mad friends, the moon does not
come back just to knock our dim efforts,

nor does the river bend away. Wasn't it
this time last year? Remember?
The chubby invitation come soon, soon

each early autumn. Look at the water
with the light jingling like a wind chime
in the shimmer. Turn around.

Our hearts   shine late   in the trees.

FEARLESS

for Moombi, Goddess & Creator of the Earth

Good to see the green world
undiscouraged, the green fire
bounding back every spring—and beyond
the tyranny of thumbs: the weeds
and other co-conspiring green genes
ganging up, breaking in, despite
small shears and kill-mowers,
ground gougers, seed eaters.
Here they come, sudden as graffiti

not there and then   there—
naked, unhumble, unrequitedly green—
growing as if they would be trees
on any unmanned patch of earth,
any sidewalk cracked, crooning
between ties on lonesome railroad tracks.
And moss, the shyest green citizen
anywhere, tiptoeing the trunk
in the damp shade of an oak.

Clear a quick swatch of dirt
and come back sooner than later
to find the green friends moved in:
their pitched tents, the first bright leaves
hitched to the sun, new roots tuning
the subterranean flavors, chlorophyll
setting a feast of light.

Is it possible   to be so glad?
The shoots rising in spite of every plot
against them. Every chemical stupidity,
every burned field, all the *Better
Homes & Gardens* finally overrun
by the green will, the green greenness

of green things growing greener.
The mad Earth publishing
her many million murmuring
unsaids. Look

how the shade pours
from the big branches—the ground
the good ground, pubic
and sweet. The trees—who
are they? Their stillness, that
long silence, the never
running away.

VISIONS

after Stephen Dobyns

These are the last days of summer.
The sky, the cool colors of sunset
make you think of things you had
wanted to do in July, but put off
till August   and now September
leans against the screen door
like the sort of friend you try
to avoid, but who catches your eye,
waves and comes in.

   A man and his cat step outside.
The cat says *I don know ablout you, but
I'm ablout ready to kick someblody in the ass.*
This is the way cats confront the weight
of broken promises and hardened injustice.
However, from his position—one hand
on the railing, the ghost-like shadow
of an oak branch grabbing his shoulder—
the man sees how flimsy his life has
become. His aching wishes that
dwarfed the city when he was young
now scrattle and ratch like dead leaves
in a schoolyard.

   The cat says *All these
sultry sallies out here and don noblody
wanna help my mojo grow? I got 6 inches
a' bulgin' hala-lula that say someblody's
glonna get religion and pretty damn soon!*
The cat believes in sex and the healing power
of conjoined flesh. He believes the right
kiss could relieve the tongue glitch
that dribbles Ls all over his speech.

124

Across the street
outside the 7-Eleven, the man sees a woman
in cut-off jeans. "Like Mary a little bit,"
he mutters, "her hair curls a little like Mary's."
He remembers certain nights—her apartment,
the almost musical refrain of her hips, the delicious
way they had fit together, pleasure swelling the room
like the smell of good cooking. But it's been years
since he's touched her or even heard her voice, so
what about all those wonderful shapes they'd made?

And for a moment he saw himself from a distance:
standing on the porch, the tree shadow
striping his brown slacks through the railing.
Like a detail you'd catch in a novel, he thinks,
the story of someone beginning to be older
than younger. "I feel so many feelings,"
he sighs, blinking at the furry blockhead
of the tom. "Like a thousand grudges, like
lemmings filling the first foot of air off a cliff—
some twisting with regret, some glad, some…"

     If the cat
could roll his eyes   he would. *Let's go
ovler to the rich neighblorhood and jus
tear shit up. Let's hurt white people
for no applarent reason.* "Aw,
shut up," the man spits.

In the man's mind he is flying,
a superhero suddenly soaring
across orchards and seas. He's
the Green Lantern, and as night
inks out day, he watches cities flare up—
the streetlamps, then Burger Kings,
billboards, neon marquees downtown.

In his eyes, the kazillion headlights
lace the whole globe in pale gold. It looks
like a thing someone might have given
as a gift, a planet made for luck—
an amulet the size of a world
dangling from Athena's dark wrist.

　　You
can kiss my flurry ass, the cat sneers. *I'm*
glonna get me a Bludweiser. *Then*
I'm'a piss on your sneaklers.
But the man wants to know why
living is almost always only slightly
bearable. How had he come to the point
where every day left him swooning like
some chump trapped in a gas station bathroom?
And what did Martin Luther King mean
when he said he'd "seen the Promised Land"?

Where had he seen it? Where did it go?

The man tries to picture *the mountain top*—
the huge maples spreading their perfect
purple shade, citizens flaunting only
their fine skins—a place where anybody
might kiss anybody anytime anybody wanted.
"But that's not it really," he says biting his
bottom lip. "There'd be time to disagree."
He didn't want a bunch of naked people
smiling everywhere. He just
didn't want it all to seem
so fuckin insane!

The man mashes his hand against his forehead
as if microscopic commandos are needling
teeny-weeny bayonets into his brain. He's
just about ready　to make somebody pay

but the cat bumps his brown head
against the man's shin *Hey,*
let's hang out on the couch. Let's glo get some
tuna flish and check out some TV. Let's watch
Bill Closby till our skulls collapse.

So that's what they do.
And that's where the man's landlord finds him
days later, staring at the luminous screen
as if into the mouth of God, the mouth
where all the beautiful visions are kept, visions
of what to eat and which computer seems more
personal, which douche is *pH-balanced,* and what trucks
are built *Ford Tough,* visions showing why
every morning you haul yourself up
and which ice-brewed beer owns the night, visions
of what's on next   and why you'll like it.

AMBITION

II.   Mosquito in the Mist

You human types, you
two-legged sapien sapiens,
you guys are like walking smoothies
ta me, milkshakes wearin trousers,
a cup'a coffee mowin the lawn.

I gotta hand it to you though—
all the colors, the smells, tall,
petite, skinny-minnies or whopping
whale-sized motha'Humphreys—you
got variety: I'm zippin around
some summa nights and it's like
an all-you-can-eat situation.

And I dig the threads—hip-hop
baggies, halter tops, baseball caps,
culottes—stylin! And
most'a the fabrics flexible enough
for me and my little straw.

But I sense some chronic
unfriendliness, some ongoing
agitation from you hemoglobes.
My family and me are small things
tryin'a quench a thirst. It's our nature.
The random violence is really
uncalled for. The bashing, the swatting—
and the *cursing!* Fuck you guys, man!
It's like you never heard'a the word
compromise.

And the worst
is when you bring down the curtain
right in the middle

of a good suck. I don't think
I need ta spotlight the obvious
analogy, but OK: imagine yourself
alone wit someone you want
real bad—*her skin is toffee,*
his hair is an avalanche
of dreadlocks—and the moment
comes: the shared
shimmer in the eyes and you
lean into the kiss, warm
and rich as God's
good cocoa, your mouth's
famished apparatus
slurping up the sweetness

when straight from hell
a smack big as Godzilla
knocks the livin
jujy-fruit outta you.

The luscious touches,
the hum of two hearts,
the holy communion flung
into the fat-ass dark forever.
What?—you think we ain't
got *feelings*?! I got the memories.
It's all in the genes! See,
you big-head motha'Humphreys
don't never think nothin
about other kinds'a life

but that's ahight: I got dreams.
I got *big* plans. I'm all itchy and bumpy
wit discontent. And you might not
see it, but I'm gettin bigger—I
been liftin—and someday I'm'a
get a little payback on the go:

land on your cheek like a
roundhouse kick, and before
you can pick up your nostrils
I'm gonna drink you dry, drain ya
to the lees: you'll be layin there
stiff as beef jerky, your arrogant
balloon all flat and wrinkly
while I lift off like a—like a

helicopter, like a goddam
12-cylinda angel, like a bulldozer
witta probiskamus—big
as a elephant's dick!

THE FURTHER ADVENTURES
OF TOOTER TURTLE

Treasent-treasent Treezle-troam
Time for this one to come home

After all I have told you, Tutah,
are you sure you want to be *black* in America?

> Well, gee, Mister Wizard, times have changed.
> It might be a little rough, but I'll be down
> with the brothaz—they'll show me the ropes.

But, Tutah, look: the republicans are on the rampage,
white people, in general, seem like dangerous playmates
and the black community is riddled with   with
self-inflicted wounds!

> Yet and still, Mr. Wizard, I would be African American.
> I've read about Fannie Lou Hamer and Malcolm.
> Black people are bold and resilient and I wanna *be* one.

> I wanna *raise up* like Michael Jordan and blow jazz
> with Wynton's quintet and   and

What, Tutah, WHAT?

> And *I wants to get funked up*, Mr. Wizard—*P-funk:*
> *The BOMB!*

Alright, Tutah, remember *if you hear any noise*
it's just me and the boys...

> {the incantation:

> > Two parts laugh and three parts pain
> > Cutting lash and hard-won gain

Thumpin bass and rumble drums
Dr. King and drive-by guns

Skin of dark and spark of eye
Sade's grace and Pippen's glide

Purple Heart and might of back

Time for Tutor   to   be   BLACK!

{Tutor, transformed, disappears into America.
Ten minutes pass:

HELP, MISTER WIZARD!!!

WELCOME HOME

after Stephen Dobyns

A terrible keening, a collective snarl arose
from the cities and plantations of the world
and White People, weary of protests and searing
rebuke, simply vanished to the moon.

They were still itchy for conquest, but their burden
had become immense; they felt under-
appreciated, even flatly despised. Sociology
dogged their steps. History betrayed them:

A little rape here…a little genocide there…

At first, everybody tried to act normal—
Whazzup, brah? Es todo, ese.
But without the wide awning of whiteness
the sky reopened like a Nigerian bazaar.

People began to dawdle before mirrors,
to lollygag around store windows: inexplicably
their complexions seemed lighter.

The global blizzard under which whole
villages had been buried, whole civilizations
lost   was finally over and marigolds
blazed all over the dark citizen rainbow.

The huge white hand that had been day and night
squeezing their heads was gone and everybody
turned off their TVs. Why watch police shows?
Why screw around with self-hatred and

dumb distraction. Gang members gave up
their automatics and started glee clubs.
Ministers admitted they knew nothing about God

and began to breastfeed in public
to prove they were starting over. Everywhere bars
closed down. Drug dealers slashed
prices but finally had to think in terms of tofu.

Without whites and the triple psychosis
"color gives privilege gives power,"
everyone started untying their shoes.
No more *Tums*, no more *Tylenol*.
No more mashing two faces into one.

Those who had spent their lives trying
to be white   whapped each other
with blobs of pizza dough and started
12-step recoveries. Each meeting
started with a chorus of *I like this ol
skin a'mine   and I'm gonna let it shine.*

After nine months the Black Separatists reacted:
they held rallies, displayed white mannequins
in hostile poses, passed out *Remember
Rodney King* billy clubs. They took over government,
sharing control with the Latin-Asian assembly.

A new draft was begun to induct those
who would pretend to be members
of the KuKluxKlan—unlucky people forced
to wear pointy hoods and shout *"Amurrika
fer Amurrikans"* and *"Ah sher as hayul
hate me some melon-eatin porch monkeys!"*

Eventually, the Nation of Islam seized power
and, with AIM soldiers as allies, ran around
sloshing nonbelievers with white paint.
"You're one filthy Caucasoid," they'd sneer,
tugging at their bowties.

"Quit messin up our threads," people smiled.
"The world is a symphony. Our lives
are the music." For without White Supremacy
and its soul-eating whispers, the old rage
that had simmered everywhere
like crocodile soup   was covered
with foil and stuffed in the fridge.

The *shop-till-you-drop* frenzy
intended to make people forget
the ruthless parade quickly sputtered.
A rash of multicultural lovefests
swept the globe: Ugandans grooving
with Filipinos while the Apache covered
their Inuit cousins with butterfly kisses.

In the third *Year of Ease*,
with the help of Colon Powell
and a few other republicans of color,
a coalition of corporate types seeped
into office. Donning Armani suits
they shuttled to the moon and found
The Whites sitting around, listless,
blending into the pale landscape.

With time on their hands like a stain
and no egg foo young and no one
to teach them how to rap, the adults
had grown somber. "Perhaps we went
too far," they nodded. "That stuff
with the Indians...those bombs
on Japan...We did get a little crazy
with the   *slavery thing.*"
Their children scowled, "What on Earth
were you thinking—it's no fun on the moon!"

The Rainbow Business Coalition
asked around until the leader, Bob Robertson—
an international televangelist—waved his hand.
He'd made a fortune dealing Krugerrands
and sat fondling a crucifix.

"We just happened to be in the area,"
the RBC said. "Figured you might need
a change of scenery, maybe some tacos?"
Bob breathed hotly, buffed the cross on his vest.
They felt awkward. Juan Valdez hummed
a little blues. "It'd sure be nice," Colon shuffled,
"to have hockey again."

"Affirmative action—*assmirmative action,*"
Justice Tommy added. "After all, what else
are bootstraps for?!"

"Hay-lay-loodoo," Bob sang, "let me pow-wow
with the others."
                    Back on Earth, the RBC
argued and begged, invoked Buddha and Jesus,
infiltrated the Baha'is, sent their faithful
door-to-door. "Imagine being white,"
they sighed, "and nobody likes you—
just because of that. Ha-lay-loodoo! Friend,
prejudice is pus in the heart!"

After a year's debate a kind of probation
was set up. Jobs would be created or
"workfare" required for those of
lunar descent. No more teams
named *Redskins,* etc. No more
Pat Boone covering *Little
Richard,* etc. A snowy day
in July would be set aside for the
celebration of White History.

This is how they returned:

First, the weather was adjusted, cooled.
Madonna, Elvis, Frank Sinatra, and The Stones
were smuggled back into music stores.
VO5 and *Cosmopolitan* were back
on the racks. Billboards offering one
well-dressed, red-haired, smiling
Caucasian sprang up with the caption:

"When you see someone *white*
do not be alarmed. This is only
a *test*. Celebrate *diversity.*"

The preparations went on and on
until, by the seventh spring, people
began to suspect the whole thing
had been a hoax, that maybe *whiteness*
itself was a myth. It was hard to
recall   what it was like with them
in the world. Maybe it hadn't been
so bad. Maybe they were too terrible
to be clearly remembered.

Then came a shining in the air, a soft
switch in the wind, a stillness as though
before a sneeze. And whites began
to fall from the sky—in a spotty drizzle
at first—a girl scout, two skiers—
then a steady shower, then a deluge
of White People. Whole suburbs
and villages, entire nations—the heavens,
like a celestial Europe, opened up.

And as the new light flickered
on the Dutch, the Spaniards, the
brown-haired Slavs, the bright-eyed

Brits   and finally, on the complicated faces
of those who'd become *American*,

the inhabitants of Earth
cried out, lifting their arms
to catch the strange, familiar bodies.

REFUGEE

Landed.　Here.

My brown skin　like a noise.

Between two mouths

a Temple: one kiss

and I have no name.　I give it

away.　I step

out of an hour: wait for The House

in my blood

to open

NOT SPOKEN

As if thirst were not a wound
As if the thirst for company were not a wound.

Consciousness   the one shadow
from which light grows.

As if all the ache flowed from the same bruise.

Near dawn. My blood caught in its circle:
I think of your body   your legs opening

and the light hairs strung along your wrists.

As if your shoulders.
As if the muscular turn of your hips.
As if I could tilt your mouth
to this dent in my chest.

So bit by bit, it becomes unmistakable.
This not knowing   how to say.

As if I had already broken
into the last room   and found the words
still not English.

As if being flesh were not call enough.

Why stay here to be American?

Where what is exactly sexual   has no country.

Let's go.
Whole words. Whole worlds slow

between us. Trying to pronounce themselves.
Unlost.

The body: the one sacred book.

My hand. My hands know
so little of your hands.

The names of pleasure   held

in chains   taken in ships.

AMBITION

III.   Primate, Bipedal

This: to find no distance
between what I am and what I seem.
To catch myself between myself

and the mirror   unafraid—
afraid of everything, *everything*.
To not have History
scaling my face.

To break the thumbs
that hung the world. To tear those hands
with these dull teeth. Human

almost. To hate. To reason. To burn
while the Sphinx feathers my ear

saying   saying *who   are you   talking to?*

This: to be pure
animal—my blood unlocked,
my legs

scribbled with hair, my soul
perched on my shoulder. Free.
Unconvinced   of my name: on my tongue
for the first time, salt.

This. I want *this*
to be my life: to come back

with my mouth ready
to send new noise.
To learn again

how to stand, how to put one foot
down   then the other a little farther along

AFTER AWHILE

for Haumea, Goddess of Love & Sexuality

And wasn't the wind   wet like April,
late April—rain blown from the bell
of a blue clarinet.

And Her hair! The dark
guitar of it   and later, the long legs
of sunlight uncrossed

but *unseen*—such instruments!

So many mad edges made into music:

Her arms open   like a storm.
If I didn't want so much
so much, why would I ever

say anything? My heart takes the corner
on two wheels: Her slow walk slow enough

to see by. My mouth harps
and harps, but what

language   is this? Dumb notes
in a dumb key. I flame
and I fizzle.

Why am I so sickly and tame?
Even now, Her hips play the world.
Bring my voice! I should praise

like a sax. I should stage
the essential noise—

as if any minute I could die
and the days would forget me.

Isn't it just   a matter of time
till somebody stutters S-
S-Seibles   *is dead.*

I'm already dead.
My life looks for itself in the windows.

And what will I do after'while?—
10,000 years with all these
almost-words still tied in my throat.

Her hair. The strum-drunken tongue
of my heart—always Her eyes: always
so undarkably dark.

IN A GLANCE

I'm caught in this curling energy! Your hair!
Whoever's calm and sensible is insane!
                                                    —Rumi

The unseeable   seen!—that saxophone
spilling from the window—a true *very soon*

held between two lips: Her smile, for no reason
a carnival quietly placed   a flaze
made to bathe in—the right door gliding
belightedly up the boulevard:

all day my heart face down my pulse
pecking like a chickadee sick of its
short wings, I had hoped some astonishing

would scratch the gravel from my eyes:
sunset hatched from a soup can, a tree toad
tap dancing with a tadpole—perhaps
a meat flag fricasseed above

my dumb country   but never the burning wheel
of a slow hour: Her smile   a glassblown *yes*
two maybes dressed in a wish—three buttercups

in a jade vase under a blue umbrella
a cello ablaze with me drawing myself
across the strings Her smile plays:

To feel so much! But not go mad enough
to shuck the grave in my skull, to scrub
and bumble for the glum Puppeteer

while my heart my teeth my
orthopedic verbs strain
like mice in a scrum

My voice!—bruised and shoeless—
goes mumbling the streets
trying to buy a vowel

My alphabet used to be ten feet long—
every letter a xylophone a shark's leg
a flubber ballooning my whole soul a holler
from the blind church of the unsaid, Her smile:

sly melody glad enough to fling the grass afire
kind season that rings the light beyond Her lips

But soft! Me, a man collided—the both the between,

the lovely shape of a mind unshaved by reason—
over the over   banging into the change

FIRST KISS

for Lips

Her mouth
fell into my mouth
like a summer snow, like a
fifth season, like a fresh Eden,

like Eden when Eve made God
whimper with the liquid
tilt of her hips—

her kiss   hurt like that—
I mean, it was as if she'd mixed
the sweat of an angel
with the taste of a tangerine,
I swear. My mouth

had been a helmet forever
greased with secrets, my mouth
a dead-end street a little bit
lit by teeth—my heart, a clam
slammed shut at the bottom of a dark

but her mouth pulled up
like a baby-blue Cadillac
packed with canaries driven
by a toucan—I swear

those lips said bright
wings when we kissed, wild
and precise—as if she were
teaching a seahorse to speak—
her mouth   so careful, chumming
the first vowel from my throat

until my brain was a piano
banged loud, hammered like that—

it was like, I swear   her tongue
was Saturn's seventh moon—
hot like that, hot
and cold and circling

circling, turning me
into a glad planet—
sun on one side, night pouring
her slow hand over the other: one fire

flying the kite of another.
Her kiss, I swear—if the Great
Mother   rushed open the moon
like a gift and you were there
to feel your shadow finally
unhooked from your wrist.

That'd be it, but even sweeter—
like a riot of peg-legged priests
on pogo sticks: up and up,
this way and higher, not
falling but on and on
like that, badly behaved
but holy—I swear! That

kiss: both lips utterly committed
to the world   like a Peace Corps,
like a free store, forever and always
a new city—no locks, no walls, just
doors—like that, I swear,
like that.

SOMEONE ELSE

She wore a long dress, twilight blue
and buttoned down the back, black buttons
sewn with yellow thread   and new sandals
and the air dozed: warm, early May, early evening—
the day about an hour from dusk.

And she had a long stride. You could tell
she worked somewhere that made her
move quickly, but now she had showered
and come outside   eating a cookie, oatmeal

raisin, and as she slipped one curved edge
between her teeth, you were nervous
about what you might say. You believed
that words could be important, that

certain sentences could change
the space between you and this
one woman   until something
had to touch. It's funny:

just before Easter she had shared a table
with a man who probably taught algebra.
The café was crowded. Twice their knees
had brushed. The page he leaned over

held difficult equations. She started
skimming her ankle along his shin
until she found herself wet. There was
something about the dare in doing it

without permission, without his ever
looking up and, to be honest, you also knew
that speaking was usually a cool fidget,
a fig leaf: you simply wanted to kiss her,

her legs that you had seen last Saturday
in shorts. Without a word, you wished
you could press your lips to her legs
to feel the muscles flex and settle—
if only once—against your mouth.

And you thought, for a second, she might
be wearing nothing but her something-
like-cinnamon smell underneath that dress

which takes you back to the once
upon a time   when you were young enough
not to know what to do with what you wanted:

one night late   the laundry room   quiet
except for the spinning dryer. Lucinda

sat on a *Maytag*, unknotted the drawstring
of her baggy plaid pajamas, and dared you—
put your mouth   right here—so you did it

kissed open the caramel flower with your
scared lips   while room by room above you
the dormitory studied and slept.

In fact, this woman, *Ms. Long Stride*,
had also been thinking about sex,
about the way her first lover didn't take

her underwear off, but tugged them
to one side with two fingers, untying
the hour with his kind hands.

And that easy sleep afterward
when she would close her eyes to the surge
and fade of five o'clock traffic: the connection
between her and the ever-raging scramble

broken   under the sumptuous weight
of good company. And at times
you have believed the sexual world

was made for this, for traveling
to exactly what you mean, across
the long separateness, the racked
stammers   into the body's only passages.

So you thought you should
say something   if there was a chance
to become more than a stranger—
though your strangeness, like everyone's,

is all you really have. There are
the loving illusions of being familiar,
of entering *a relationship*—and words
do make the boundaries

less definite, make it almost possible
to understand someone else, to see
someone composing himself
between inflection and breath

meaning to say how it is
what it is   and why
this *wanting* equals
what it does.

Instead, you asked her the time
and stumbled some dumb song about
warm weather and summer coming.

And she was thinking things too, showing
the watch on her wrist   and the careful
reach of her voice, her own odd history
telling her   what not to say.

Once, at a birthday party where you
turned 39, a good friend sat on the sofa
slyly revealing the flimsy underwear she wore.

One knee would drift away from the other
and she'd laugh—the soft gloss of purple silk
barely lit by the lamp in the corner.

And later you lay in her bed watching her
take off your pants in the wall-sized mirror,
watching how, with her lips wet, she

leaned over the slight curve of your cock
and you saw your face for a second
given back by the glass,

so you *were* someone else, being there,
her legs around you, her body
repeating its luminous phrase
as if to clarify everything.

You understood then   that *this*
is what would blaze inside your skull

years after your life was over: that ache,
her mouth, the nearly spoken—

moments when your body became
an invitation, a window, a way to admit

the weary angels: other people, the one
inscrutable word   rushing into your arms.

LATE SHIFT

Places—
maybe dreams

from which I cannot   return: the velvet

touch of first light
fingering a cup: sacred dislocations

of mind—the way the right sound
becomes visible

Where I am now
it's later: the clocks have been amended

to include all the strange hours—

and Someone cracked my name
as if all my life I'd been locked inside.

I know the shelves stay stocked, big cars
lead the chase, there's always more

and more to eat   but was that ever
my country?

I was   born there.
And I'd go back if I could,

but what I took to be a certain distance

was actually a late   shift in myself:

a different kind of listening—
the voice, a thread of honey

the jar tipped just enough to one side.

Listen.

We belong to no nation.

One day we will hold the Earth
again   as if She'd been a love

nearly lost, Her rainy hair tangled
in our hands.

The soul is what we are.
Every life a word the wind turns to say.

And though trouble
grows back like a beard,

an unchained blood governs my tongue.

I have seen the door   that is not there

still open

from *FAST ANIMAL* (2012)

And petals falling to the floor
from the wound in my head...

—Ai

BORN

Is this
how it begins:

a cry that
does not know

who's crying: consciousness
filling your head

like smoke—the brain
a burning house—

first surge of *self*
as a thing

apart: scorched,
the shock

of touch, smell
and somehow

hunger: the need
to have

what you
cannot have

without help—the
unintentional world

wayward,
aloof—then maybe

relief
in someone's arms: is

this
where your heart rises

then tilts:
between hunger

and

the moment
you are fed—

the mind sprung
by want—your mouth:

the first taste, the forgetting

where you are
and what's to come

4 A.M.

I caught the last great caravan of clouds.
City night. Sky like the inside of a skillet

and bright as ghosts, they crossed—not slowly
but unhurried—as if remembering the way

by feel, the way you might touch the wall
of a dark hall at a friend's house late, moving

toward the back porch where you heard the June bugs
unbuttoning their brass jackets. September.

September: another good summer gone and me
another season older with these streets

wet from a small storm that woke me
to see silver clouds drawn along the sky.

But before that   I had been dreaming: a box
of bottles on the back seat of a car, sunlight

sassing the windshield. A hitchhiker
wearing the bluest baseball cap

you ever saw. I guess I had been
driving and somehow money

was involved, but neither of us knew
how much. We knew the police

were hiding inside the church. "But look
how it is," he said, "The road,

I mean, and wide," and the wind stuttered
in the spidery weeds while the asphalt stirred

like a dark sheet under which someone
sleeping had turned over and then

it *was* a river   much wider than a road,
with the air barely brushing the trees

the way you might touch the hair of someone
you loved once, stumbling into her

beneath the marquee after a movie. It was
hard smiling the brief embrace, seeing her walk

away, because her walk was the reason
you had tried to meet her five Junes ago—

her smiling voice, the almost sleepy grace
in her gait. You remember scolding yourself

for *wanting* again: you already believed
she would pass through your life—

which she did—like the good season
of a late hour, like a brightness

opening the dark by feel,
the way a blindfolded boy looks

for his friends in his unlit basement—
the quiet so thick he begins to think

they are gone completely   which, in fact
they are: having one by one

slipped out the back door
where after some giggles

they catch the sunset
rubbing brass into their blue jackets

and decide   to just go home
while he traces the walls,

the dusty sofa, the smooth plank
of the ironing board, not knowing his hands

would eventually find the differences
between what moves what stays and what

was never really there at all.

NOTES FROM BIG BRAH, TOM THE BOMB

Don Juan of Germantown High School, 1967–68

I say, Tom,
there's this girl—

> *He says, Is she fine like apple wine?*
> *She fine enough to be a friend a'mine?*

Her name is Tina—

> *So you wanna give Tina ya weena?*

and Doc's havin a party—

> *Is she tuned to your station?*
> *She believin what you fakin?*

and she's gonna be there—

> *Tell'er you know the way*
> *to San Jose   Tell'er*
> *you gotta graze in her grass.*

> *Tell'er you   ♫ ain't too proud to beg ♫*

> *Yeah, ya gotsta Rock Hudson on'er.*
> *Give'er the movie-star moon gazer—*
> *the look of love—say, "My duty*
> *is   your bootie."*

> *Tell'er your peter is sweeter*
> *and ya know how to treat'er.*

> *Ya gotta sing a little bittle, little brother,*
> *Gotsta hit'er witta little bitta Sinatra:*

> *♫ Everybody*
> *loves my body   sometime... ♫*

TERRY MOORE

Our moms got us together at Woolworth's,
remember? Cheeseburgers. Summertime, 1967:
twelve years in the world. Mostly we burned

for football, to get it and move, to shake anybody
that wanted to bring us down—six points
was all we needed and time to find the future

where we'd be badass superstars. We thought
it was hard being young with adults everywhere
and it got harder   not to think about girls

and which words would bring them close
to our hands. Miniskirts: remember *checkin*
the cheese in study hall—Marna Evans—

we had no idea where those legs could lead.
If it weren't for movies and the legends
of our big brothers we might never have believed

in smooth whispers, long kisses, and maybe even now
we'd be dreaming only football—the rough touch
of leather grabbed and carried to a place

where men danced with nothing to explain:
the endzone, the promised land—and who could
blame us for craving such a simple destination?

Then came Joanie, and for me it was Jane. Short hugs,
slow songs, their mouths swimming into our mouths.
Among the Philly brothers, the word was *swag*.

Did you swag on'er? we'd ask, supposing the wet
dream of lips. How many times did y'all swag: so new
the French kiss, the perfect neighborhood for anyone

as crazy and blue-balled as boys blazing
on the verge of the verge of their lives.

Man, we spent years on the phone daring each other
not to be young, not to be afraid of whatever sex
might mean. That paperback you found, *Nurse*

Nadine—the way she treated her patients. (What
exactly was a *blowjob*   and how long would it be
till we knew?) Our fathers were scary men, younger

than we are now—and ready to make themselves clear
without saying anything, especially when we got too cool
to listen, too big to hear. Did they believe in sex

the way we were starting to? Was there some secret living
softly inside their fists? My father loved my mother.
It looked so simple: year after year, the kiss

goodbye after breakfast, the kiss hello about five,
conversation at dinner, TV until time for bed.
It's pretty clear   I didn't know much

about my parents—just that they were usually
nice people and mostly on my side—and this
makes me wonder just how blind I'm gonna be

'cause these days, I hardly see anything
the way I saw things back then   and, brah,
my eyes are wide open. The NFL will never

see us: I can't do half the moves we used to do—
loose-leg lean, that cutback stutter: short grass
lit beneath our simmering feet. But I'm glad

these forty years have found us still friends,
that we played some football and watched each other
break slowly into men   which is what we are by now—

which was always what we thought we really wanted.

WOUND

Door
in the flesh
leading where: what

exactly does pain
teach? As if time always

lived in the mirror
as if the past
itself   looked back—
I remember

what they did: I keep
remembering
the way consciousness
turned

like a fast animal
to the blood
on my face: being

awake
suddenly meant something
else. My eyes

for a second,
caught the hidden
slant   and whatever
happened before

that
also changed

MAD POETS VILLANELLE

The sunrise is nice, but the nightside is bad
When light breaks the dawn, a black sky turns blue
I think I know why certain poets go mad

I once rode the cosmos in a suit stitched in plaid
The Earth was my spaceship and me, the rough crew
The big light was nice, but the nightside was bad

I can't understand why I can't understand
They learned me some books and their churchery too
It's pretty damn clear why the poets turn mad

It's a bootieful life! Shouldn't sex make us glad?
But the first touch of lips brings the turn of the screw
The first light's good light, but the blindside is bad

Be all you can be like it says in the ad
And do a few things that the Janjaweed do
You can see why the sweet poets run mad

Sometimes I think I've been totally had
I fell for this life 'cause I thought life was true
The daylight's alright, but the sunset is sad

It looks like this chance is all that I had
I say to the mirror *That just can't be you*
I guess I see why half the people go mad

Maybe if I could just talk to my Dad:
Didn't you think that your dream would come true?
The sunrise is nice, but the blindside is bad
I think I know why certain poets go mad

VENDETTA, MAY 2006

My thoughts are murder to the State and
involuntarily go plotting against her.
                              —Henry David Thoreau

As if leaving
it behind would
have me lost
in this place, as if

keeping it
could somehow
save me from the
parade of knives,

I have held
my rage on a short
leash like a good
mad dog whose bright

teeth could keep
the faces of our enemies
well lit. Is it

wrong to hate
the leaders? Am I wrong
to hate their red

ties and their
secret economies?
Am I wrong? Am I?

Look how they
work the stage
like cool comedians,

ribbing the nations this
way, then that—
gaff after giggle

filling the auditoriums
with the empty
skulls. Maybe this

is the moment
to abandon
metaphor: shouldn't somebody
make *them*

suffer: now that
war is easy money
won't the reasons
keep coming to see

how well
people die? I guess
this
is the world

I was born
into. I remember
the first time I saw

autumn outside
my window: the colors

came with the smell
of burning

leaves   and starving
in our basement,

the crickets
tried to stave off

the chill, still working
their little whistles
after dark.

I think, even
then, I knew

a season
would come

for us: the wind
tilting slowly

until everyone
is under the cold
still holding on
to their wallets

as the government
steadily turns   and day

after day, the terrible stories
cover everything.

Years ago, a pregnant woman was bitten by a vampire and turned.
Her son was born with the thirst, but being half-human, he could walk
in sunlight unharmed. Though vampires still dominate the world, he
fights them—in part to avenge his long isolation, being neither human
nor vampire. Because of his deadly expertise and weapon of choice
they call him:

BLADE, THE DAYWALKER

Like a stake
in my heart: this life—

the seen
the unseen—the ones

who look in the mirror
and find nothing

but innocence   though they stand
in blood up to their knees.

You see them: shadows

not shadows, people who seem

to be people. You don't
believe me? I watch

their news, drink coffee
in their chains.

There's no place
they haven't touched:

it's almost like I can't
wake up, like I'm living

in a movie, a kind of dream:
action-packed thriller.

I never
dreamed this

hunger in my veins, this
mind that cannot sleep: why

do I whet this blade
when they will not die?

EDGE

Traffic: solitude—
the city walking around.

So many of us lost in it.
Is love the secret

nobody tells? In a small park
daylight pulled its knife

and a tree moved
toward me: *What are you*

doing here?
I remembered then: I lit

my eyes which had
gone out

ODE TO MY HANDS

Five-legged pocket spiders, knuckled
starfish, grabbers of forks, why
do I forget that you love me:
your willingness to button my shirts,
tie my shoes—even scratch my head!
which throbs like a traffic jam, each thought
leaning on its horn. I see you

waiting anyplace always
at the ends of my arms—for the doctor,
for the movie to begin, for
freedom—so silent, such
patience! testing the world
with your bold myopia: faithful,
ready to reach out at my
softest suggestion, to fly up
like two birds when I speak, two
brown thrashers brandishing verbs
like twigs in your beaks, lifting
my speech the way pepper springs
the tongue from slumber. O!

If only people knew the unrestrained
innocence of your intentions,
each finger a cappella, singing
a song that rings like rain
before it falls—that never falls!
Such harmony: the bass thumb, the
pinkie's soprano, the three tenors
in between: kind quintet x 2,
rowing my heart like a little boat
upon whose wooden seat I sit
strummed by sorrow. Or maybe

I misread you completely
and you are dreaming a tangerine, one

particular hot tamale, a fabulous
banana! to peel suggestively
like thigh-high stockings: grinning
as only hands can grin
down the legs—caramel, cocoa,
black-bean black, vanilla—such lubricious
dimensions, such public secrets!
Women sailing the streets

with God's breath at their backs.
Think of it! No! *Yes*:
let my brain sweat, make my
veins whimper: without you, my five-hearted
fiends, my five-headed hydras, what
of my mischievous history? The possibilities
suddenly impossible—feelings
not felt, rememberings un-
remembered—all the touches
untouched: the gallant strain

of a pilfered ant, tiny muscles
flexed with fight, the gritty
sidewalk slapped after a slip, the pulled
weed, the plucked flower—a buttercup!
held beneath Dawn's chin—the purest kiss,
the caught grasshopper's kick, honey,
chalk, charcoal, the solos teased
from guitar. Once, I played
viola for a year and never stopped

to thank you—my two angry sisters,
my two hungry men—but you knew
I just wanted to know
what the strings would say
concerning my soul, my whelming
solipsism: this perpetual solstice
where one + one = everything
and two hands teach a dawdler
the palpable alchemy
of an unreasonable world.

BLADE, HISTORICAL

*It is possible that God exists, but with everything
that has happened to us, could it possibly matter?*
                    —Mario Vargas Llosa

You come into the world—
from where *from where*—
and the world turns

toward you, fangs bared,
disguised as what it is, as if
this is how it has to be:

as if it were normal to walk
the daylight knowing
something's wrong. *Grow up,*

they say, *get a job, go to church.*
And after a while you stop
fighting it and try to smile.

Don't you ever wonder
whose blood is in
the banks? It's yours.

Follow the money
back to The Plague and
the rise of the papacy:

The Inquisition. *The Burning
Times.* The explorers
and the *explored.* So many

centuries, so much
death: you can still taste it
on the wind. Some days

I think, with the singing
of my blade, I can fix
everything—even the sadness

that says nothing that matters
will change. Some days
I think I should never have been.

ALLISON WOLFF

Like a river at night, her hair—
the sky starless, streetlights
glossing the full dark of it:
Was she Jewish? I was seventeen

an "Afro-American" senior
transferred to a suburban school
that held just a few of us.
And she had light-brown eyes

and tight tube tops   and skin
white enough to read by
in a dim room. It was impossible
not to be curious.

Me and my boy, Terry, talked about
"pink babes" sometimes: we watched
I Dream of Jeannie and could see Barbara
Eden, in her skimpy finery, lounging

on our very own lonely sofas.
We wondered what white girls were
really like, as if they'd be raised
by the freckled light of the moon.

I can't remember Allison's voice
but the loud tap of her strapless heels
clacking down the halls is still clear.
Autumn, 1972: race was the elephant

sitting on everybody. Even
as a teenager, I took the weight
as part of the weather, a sort of heavy
humidity felt inside and in the streets.

One day, once upon a time, she laughed
with me in the cafeteria—something
about the Tater Tots, I guess
or the electric-blue *Jell-O*. Usually

it was just some of us displaced brothers
talkin noise, actin crazy, so she
caught all of us way off-guard. Then
after school, I waved   and she smiled

and the sun was out—that 3 o'clock
after-school sun rubbing the sidewalk
with the shadows of trees—

and while the wind pitched the last
of September, we started talking
and the dry leaves shook and sizzled.

In so many ways, I was still a child
though I wore my seventeen years
like a matador's cape.

The monsters that murdered
Emmett Till—were they *everywhere?*
I didn't know. I didn't know enough
to worry enough about the story
white people kept trying to tell.

And given the thing that America is,
maybe sometimes such stupidity works
for the good. Occasionally,

History offers a reprieve, everything
leading up to a particular moment
suddenly declared a mistrial:
so I'm a black boy suddenly

walking the Jenkintown streets
with a white girl—so ridiculously
conspicuous   we must've been
invisible. I remember her mother

not being home and cold *Coca-Cola*
in plastic cups and the delicious
length of Allison's tongue and
we knew without saying anything
we were kissing the *color line*

goodbye   and on and on for an hour
we kissed, hardly breathing, the light almost
blinding whenever we unclosed our eyes—
as if we had discovered the dreaming door
to a different country   and were walking
through it   as if we could actually

walk the glare we'd been
born into: as if my hand
on her knee, her hand
on my hand, my hand
in her hair, her mouth
on my mouth   opened
and opened and opened

WHAT

Curiosity: seed
that turns the world
into what

we are
told
by those who
were told
by still others
what's what: The
Telling—

the great storm
each man each
woman walks
as if beneath

a second sky—this
and this of course
and this—the rain

rains down
like rain
everywhere
and all over

we don't
know that
we don't

know
what's been
done to us:
consciousness

kept like a fly
in a jar, a small
hope buzzing the glass:

What is it
what—
is it, what—
what is it?

BLADE, UNSYMPATHETIC

They don't matter; they're our food.
                              —Deacon Frost

Ever take Communion? Ever
watch the war on TV? This place
is for predators, baby.
It doesn't matter
that you never knew:
your innocence

is the key they turn
to let you out
and lock you in. Nobody
wants to see
what's

really happening—
and by the time you
start to understand,
the baby teeth are gone
and the big teeth
come in: you're in
the blood

and the blood's   on you.
If you play along
almost everyone will
sort of
be your friend: in the
human world
don't the wolves look a lot
like the sheep

before the slaughter
begins? Try to remember:
Is that *your* face

in the window? Is that
your name on the card?

Maybe you should get
some body armor. What else
can I say? Mine is black.
Eat as much garlic
as you can.

FROM DARKNESS

Sunrise runs
a fresh wind through the leaves,
a night turns
back into shadows.

Waking up, the birds tell
first light
everything they know.

Why do we keep
killing each other?

The Earth is a woman

who walks
in the sky, *walks*
in the sky! Her legs
so long

you can't even see them.
For no reason, the morning comes

back again, saying *Come back—*
open your eyes.

DONNA JAMES

I remember that first time:
the empty auditorium, her voice,
the dark all around us,
her mouth reaching into mine.
She was Tony's foxy older sister
and I didn't know why
she wanted to kiss me. She
had already finished high school
and probably shouldn't have
been walking the halls, but
she always called me her *friend*.
So one Monday after gym

I found myself beside myself
in front of her house—with my
trench coat and lunch bag—
probably *not* looking much
like Shaft. Inside, the air held
warm milk and we talked a bit
about her baby and her aunt
who paid the rent painting cars.

Maybe she liked me because
we were both black and mostly
alone in the suburbs, but I hadn't
thought about that. It was her voice
that got me—banked fire the color
of dusk—her voice   and my name
was smoke in her mouth.

I think about it more than I should now,
that January noon, an hour before
algebra—how most days I'd be
thinking football   or replaying
the seventy-some kisses I'd gotten
over those lean years, but that day

Donna and me were on the couch
munching potato chips. *Rrruffles
have rrridges* she kidded, coming
from checking the baby who'd
slipped into a nap. I was kind of
disappointed that we hadn't
done anything, but I needed time
to get back to school, so I started
to stand. She said, *Wait,
look at this mess,*

and with her left hand, she
brushed the crumbs from my lap
the way you'd whisk away lint—
then swept over my pants again—
to be thorough, I guessed, but slower
and then some more, as if her hand

were getting   drowsy. You know
how sometimes you see something
but just can't believe it—like a squirrel
bobbling a biscuit on your kitchen counter
or a cricket creeping the red feathers
of your mother's Sunday hat?

Her hand *there*, on my lap
could easily have been a five-fingered
flying saucer from the fifth dimension.
For a while, I just watched and
wondered if she knew where
her hand had landed   but it was me
who didn't know, *me* with my
six dozen kisses and the great Eden
of my virginity. How
do we not talk about it

every day: the ways
we were changed
by the gift

186

in someone's touch—your body
suddenly a bright instrument
played by an otherwise
silent divinity.

When I heard my zipper, I couldn't
have said where my arms
were   or what a clock was for:
I had
no idea I could be such a stranger
and still be myself. How could I
have known what a girl

might do to a boy
with her mouth   if she felt
like doing what her mouth
could do? It was
a kind of miracle: the dreamed
impossible—my soul finally called
to my flesh. I didn't know
what I didn't know   and then I knew.

SORROW

It's not the same
as sadness, though sorrow
has sadness in it—the way *lost*

holds losing: you can see it
in women's eyes when they laugh
and in the way men lean

over their food: after a while
we know nearly every love
won't go as it should

and we know that knowing
cannot make us glad: *knowledge*
stairway to nowhere—we want

the world we cannot have
and every day the feeling moves
between us, but we try

not to complain and almost
never fall down and cry.

DANCING VILLANELLE

I guess nobody ever really stands a chance
Man, even the good guys wind up dead
But shouldn't we dance, shouldn't we dance?

I caught the mean truth in a midlife glance
The friendliest innocence is finally bled
Parents must know kids don't stand a chance

These long-legged women got me looking askance:
Is monogamy honestly better instead?
Let's all of us dance! Couldn't we dance?

I wish mom had warned me a bit in advance
For the rest of my life, I'll be face down in bed
You learn to accept that a man's got no chance

I'd like to receive a nice blowjob in France
A touch of détente to help beat back the dread
If you ask real nice won't they stand you a chance?

Suppose I show up and just take off my pants?
There's a good chance I'd get kicked in the breads
But couldn't we dance? Shouldn't we dance?

Let's work like zombies, walk malls in a trance
And buy all the bullshit they shine in our heads
Why even wake up if they won't let you dance?

I'm gripping the wheel with both of my hands
Wherever you go the clocks wring out the dead
I guess nobody ever really stood a chance
But didn't we dance, didn't we?

A SONG

from little Kathleen's note

I hope that we will meet again
if we meet again
I hope

we will meet again
if we meet
again   There was
so much

I didn't say
this time   I hope we will
meet again if we

meet again   Will day
break night again
when we meet
again

I won't be this
afraid again
when we meet
again   Won't that

be something
if we meet again
I will play again

when we
meet again if you'll
meet again   I won't
sleep again if we meet again

I hope we meet again

190

Shouldn't we
meet again
if we meet again   What
could I say

if we meet again
The water
would be sweet
again if we meet

again   Won't the trees
be tall again if we
climb again

Would it be
here again if we meet
again

Or is again
not like again
I swear

we will meet
again if we meet again
Don't you think

we'll meet
again
when we meet
again   I hope

we can meet
again   Will you
know that we've met
again if we

meet again when we
meet again   Would again

seem like again
again   I hope
we will meet again

if we meet
again once we meet
again   I hope
we will meet again

from *ONE TURN AROUND THE SUN* (2017)

Now the world is buried in me, to the hilt.

—Jenny George

ODE TO YOUR MOTHER

Do you remember yourself
six months after conception?
Far from the egg, your heart
chirping like a hungry chick,
those unwalked feet—fat crickets
kicking around, eyes blind
as buttons: cell by cell,
rod by cone, getting ready
to call up the colors and lights,

and your mother, often craving
licorice with apple pie, outside
catching a bus with you—
in her warm pond—a golden koi
nosing the surface for bits of bread,
you: the unnamed stranger
coming for the long stay,
traveling all night, your face
taking shape in the shadows

or maybe she sees herself:

a bass drum with something
booming inside her, a small theater
off-Broadway with someone soon
to be famous pacing the wings—
so much promise! Were you restless
to begin?—all your vitals rehearsing
their hard parts. Did you have any sense
that she was out there?—your brain

almost building itself: a secret
mansion—a million doors
to a million rooms, each
with a candle, your little head

holding the Milky Way
rekindled in miniature: consciousness,
The Great Mischief, waking up

to try again—one particular
flicker in the cosmic sea, a starfish
riding the big back of a blue whale—
which swims like a planet
gliding the sun's slow waves

with you   beginning to insist
inside this woman you hardly
know, though she is Everything,
steadying her new weight
on Earth. Your heart

blind as a kite—wind
on the rise, three months
from *Day*. Did you suppose
an inkling   of what would be
out there—the invisible air
filling us up, rabbits in hats,
hints, houses, banana slugs,
bacteria, and trees!
Other people—

the look
on your face   already amazed

or whatever comes
just before that.

ODE TO YOUR FATHER

Sunday nights
he put on Yusef Lateef
and that flute stole secrets
usually locked in the moon's
cool house   and you watched
his head nod *yes* to all
he couldn't say, then tiptoed
back to TV, hoping he'd forget
it was past your time for bed.

When he yelled at you
you probably heard
his father yelling at him
though you couldn't
recognize the flat "don't
talk back" settled beneath
his voice like a big bass
at the bottom of a lake.

Growing up, he said *yes sir*
to that brassy baritone and
wasn't his father's father's voice
a part of him too, that part
that seemed tied up
in some long-ago trouble,
even when he sat in the shade
baiting a hook.

Hard to picture it now: him
in his straw hat and highwater
dungarees, Oklahoma boy
moping home with a loaf of bread,
his buddies teasing and tempting him
back to the park. How did he

face his first bully?—the one
that cracked his tooth
and cut his arm. Ever wonder
where he got that
hot-grease-in-the-face glare,
the look that made you
so afraid?—his father made him
fight that tough kid twice.

And at times, didn't the whole country
try to break his skin, waiting for him
on every corner like a bully. What
did he make of all those stores
that wouldn't let him in? He worked
the slaughterhouse—stiff
with dried blood, his overalls
could stand by themselves.

In spite of this, you found him
years later: your pop mopping the kitchen,
whistling "My Satin Doll," a tune
you hadn't heard, so half-listened
as if he were some odd station
on the radio. And when he'd start

the old "things were different
back then," it sounded like *once
upon a time.* You shrugged
and secretly rolled your eyes
but half of you is still made
of him: his long arms, his love
of hats, your solitary heart: half
jazz, half ready to fight.

Your father didn't kiss you
like your mother did, but
every October he drove you
to the arboretum to see

the blood-orange leaves, even
when he had a lot on his mind.
That mind

you'll never see inside
though you know it's packed
with good songs, some hard feelings
and all the stuff he will not say.

COMPOSITE

Your weight

on one foot, then
the other:

walking—
that taste of baked
bread so bright
your mouth is born
again. December:

a coin,
cold circle
in your hand—
each

of us   made
from two people:

your body,
an angel's

tambourine—
the self, something

like lamplight
on a slush-covered
street: can

someone else

see what I mean?
Does everybody

hear that slight
ringing

WALK

Dusk in the body,
   starlight near the heart.

One half-lit street
   heading into night: now

the insects magnify
   their small vocabularies

as if talking   to you
   your shadow sharp

almost alive
   beneath the lamp.

———————

Do we live to scuff each
   hour   dragging the hours

past?—as if you could
   see best by turning back—

the Present   Her lips soft
   on your neck / the future

filling with ghosts.

I still remember
   the first dog I ever saw:

that crazy tongue, the one sound
   flashing between its teeth.

Days when *Cracker Jacks*
   crashed their music in me

and crabgrass sizzled
    with chiggers, us playing tackle

till the sun ran out of breath.
——————

Where was it
    that your heart first

opened? Where, when you first
    began to shutter its rooms?

Your mind gradually bending
    beneath the suspicion

that life   would not
    save us, that *love* itself

was little more than a hook
    for the mouth—time spent dying

quietly, driving to work.
——————

Car radio: the yammer,
    that itchy fuss, each bit

a ballpeen hammer
    chipped against your skull

and the street somehow
    miles away, the funhouse

distance   between your *self*
    and everyone else. To be awake

means what? Hearing

that voice start over
   in your head, the worries

walking in place: the argument
   backlit—*why do you*

do this? Thinking,
   thinking: your brain caught

in the swarm. Words
   telling you what not to say.

_____

I have tried to pass
   as an almost reasonable man

as if that could mean much
   these days: Cruelty showing off

His sample tray of meats.
   Have enough

people died? Has first dark
   found your shadow

in a vague circle of light?—the day
   walking off, hard news

turned rot in your mouth.
   Is it true   the mirror

has confused you
   with someone else?

_____

Maybe it is too easy
    to say *darkness* and mean

trouble or whatever it is—
    what we can't fight, what

the years do to us:

that smoldering sense
    of having been taken

prisoner, though you sit there
    almost a fly   feeding—

sunlight like sequins
    on your faceted eyes.

_____

A woman goes by with pants
    like liquid glass   and I catch myself

leaning on memory: the promise
    of people we don't

know. I have been
    a stranger: that first hour

in someone's arms

when it seems we will
    never want again—

as if touch held
    the cure to this

chronic condition: the
    half-knowing / being half

understood: this blink
    and smile, the way we go

outdoors with the other things
    held inside our faces—

so I'm older now
_____

but maybe the safest thing we can do
    is insist on what might not be

found here, this hopeful walk
    toward Neverland. I think about

Fear, its steady governance
    all over   and what people

are willing to believe
    to keep from being alone—

the mind spurred
    to build its own cage:

hatred or the hunger
    for *God*   an ache for

money—how a
    mob becomes a

country becomes the
    history   against

which   we must break
    our lives.
_____

What I've become: this
    running clock, this heretic, these

brushed teeth, this cock
    covered in cloth, this gang

of muscles wearing down,
    my brain a nest just starting

to burn: this *this*

that I carry around.
    Tell me,

wherever you are, tell me
    just how hungry we might be:

forks wet with food
    filling the opened faces

all day the daylight
    eaten.

———————

From his garage, a man
    and his hammer rattle birds

who'd been near sleep: now
    the branches chick and chatter

now the ants reconsider
    their silence   and something else

comes clear: the veins
    in the leaves are the same

in your hands—Time starts walking
    into voice—you see yourself

on a street: three miles
    before starlight, one late wasp

almost blind, climbs back
    to its place   in the eaves.

TASTE ME BLUES VILLANELLE

The Mad Hatter's tea party
is the whole fuckin world
                    —overheard

Not sure what I'm doin   and can't say where I'll be
People think they know me but don't see how I am
When they get me, I bet the germs enjoy me

I grope along this broken road from sea to shining sea
The madness roots inside me, while I revise my plans
Looks like what I'm doin might make me what I'll be

Isn't it enough we're stuck   and cannot fight or flee?
Weather burns the world of men; tornadoes walk the land
When they stop me, I hope the cops enjoy me

The time has come the Walrus said to talk at many things
I turn around to look around and try to take a stand
But don' know what I'm doin and can't say what I mean

I've always been an optimist   so that is what I'll be
I'm at your door with *Wonder Bread*, some butter and some jam
If you kiss me   I think your lips'll like me

Daylight is the splintered plank I walk into the sea
Got up with a hustle   but went down flimmed and flammed
When muthafuckas find me, they'll wonder who I be

I'm at the Hatter's Party shovin honey in my tea
The time we saved, the wage they paid felt something like a scam
When they bite me, them greenhead flies annoy me

Won't say I'm a token, but can't say I rode free
You'll catch me at the Starbucks—broken donut in my hand

Don't like where it's goin, but that's just how I'll be
When they taste me, I hope the worms enjoy me

THE HILT

Second Session

The see-saw, I remember—
 my big brother stranding me
  up in the air: the
   bright green willow, red
    ants running the trunk.
     Sunday school. This was

      behind the church. Japanese
       beetles were eating the roses.
        I wore a fake tie clipped to my
         stiff, white shirt

Having ushered you into the who-knows-what that waited in the world,
having seen your face before that first hard glint hacked your eyes,

when they look at you now, do your parents find anything familiar?

Sometimes I think
I see myself. Am I on TV?—

getting
a sandwich
starting the car
calling somebody
calling back—
bizzy.

After awhile, the sun looks
over its shoulder. *Every day*

in this window
a mannequin
turns his
perfectly
trained
face

The self is real, right?—this who-you-are, this
soft wheel: these chronic recollections—

Does it feel like a trick? This thing

you've become: some dream re-running
in your veins, what you   believe,

the way you walk—some sign
of a lifelong shove: your mind

a shy animal, force-fed, skinned

In the video

before the
police came
Tamir Rice
was a kid

playing a-
lone in a
park near
the gazebo.

I used to do that.
I'd have my football with me, a water gun in my pocket,
maybe some *Sugar Babies*.

Before the
uniform
opened
fire,

do you
think that
boy had
any idea

his story
was al-
ready
written?

Afternoons I would sit in the basement building houses with *Lego*.
Laundry hung from the pipes and when someone
opened the door, the draft made the shirts
move like ghosts.

The bones beneath my face—my mother's cheeks, my father's tough brow.
How they've added up in me: my brother and I their lengthening shadows.

Late at night, I find myself thinking like a man overboard, like someone
up to his neck:

you find yourself
trapped at a certain age,

try to move   try to gnaw through your leg:
whatever it takes—
reason against reason

So many days I'm in this coffee shop
writing to make a case for the beauty that begins and ends
with us.

In the parking lot there's this guy yelling
at everything   no one else
can see. His

pants are wrecked, his ragged afro
mostly gray. He does

not see himself   being
seen. He does not
know where he has gone.

"Death hides in the world

so we disguise ourselves"

/if we can.

Born the year of Emmett Till   as if a country could itself be a kind of

knife, I have lived with some hate   like a blade eased in and withdrawn
carefully. This is the slow way. *Your heart*

fractured like a skull   but your face seems the same, the streets look
just like streets and

look how the day burns down while you reach for a different history—
time filling the air   like sunset

ZOMBIE BLUES VILLANELLE

There are days I believe there is nothin to fear
I rev up for green lights, my engine on call
But it could be the zombies are already near

That sleep that we feed every day of the year
What's up with your friends when they circle the mall?
There are nights when I think I have no one to fear

My Mom watches *Oprah* to sweeten the year
You can keep your eyes open, see nothing at all
But it might be the zombies are already near

You think life is s'posed to be lived in this gear?
Been askin that question till my brain has gone raw
Certain days I believed I had nothing to fear

I have dreams where I'm drivin with no way to steer
You can growl like a cello; you can chat like a doll
At the games, ain't it always the zombies who cheer?

I think *fear itself* is a whole lot to fear
I watch CNN till it makes my skin crawl
I might be a zombie that's already here

I been pounding this door but don' nobody hear
You can drink till you think that you're seven feet tall
Fast dances, good chances, and nothin to fear

You can fly through your days until time is a smear
Maybe blaze up the bong or blog out a blog

There'll be days when you know you've got nothing to fear
But you could be a zombie that's already here.

AT 59

after Randall Jarrell

Roving from Nike to New Balance,
Prince to Puma, I pick up a pair
of size 13s, some shorts, and blue sweats,
still feeling the sneakered beast scuff
his muzzle against my skull.

Two tall, hard-shouldered young brothaz
fondle *Air Jordans*, talkin' a little shit:
If I getchu down on the block
wit **deez** *muhfuckas'll be callin' you* **Betty.**

"A drowning man," Mooji wrote, "is not
interested in air"—and as the constellation
that pardoned my life goes dark, I recognize
this snag in my chest, this cut breath, this

lonely, late midlife knowing: the inescapable
all around me, desperation all around—my own

stumbly efforts at love, my own
trying to say   *say something,*
while the duck-speaking dickheads
salute their zombie platoons.

Always big, bad Death posting me up,
backing me down, the ball's trick bounce
busting my brain: I know He's smooth
with either hand, but still mean
to snuff his shot.

                In my college days
when my parents were well
and the bulk of worry sat elsewhere,
I strolled around with *my boys* and mostly
we wanted the same things:

to play sports, "make big bucks," and have
the fine babes find the come-hither in our faces.

What I miss   is that damn sure *hellyeah!*
we carried like crisp cash. JC, his wit,
that manic laugh—Eric's slick grin,
and Doc, so lean only his head
cast shadow: that loud halo
of hair. "Don't touch the 'fro," he'd say.

I miss my boys and the Ohio Players
funkin' us up against the Earth's black hips—

>   *...you a bad, bad missez*
>   *with those skin-tight britches*
>   *runnin' folks into ditches, yeah...*

We couldn't help ourselves.

There's a girl: a young woman, I guess
in her mid-20s, testing the exercise machines—
a serious athlete wearing sneaks that mean
speed, her righteous gluteus maximus rippling
each lift and pull. What I wish, now that I'm
older, is that she see through the three decades
between us   and work *my* back, but these days

I'm a *sir* a gray beard to be addressed
with deference, someone whose wisdom could
maybe be vaguely revered.

O Sex, songbook of our better angels, how I craved
and savored your generous pages—chapter
and verse   and verse: kissing for hours, daylight lost
to the liquid velvet of the tongue, the body:
delicious synagogue, cello hungry to be bowed.

I don't believe the longing ever ends. I can't believe
I'll ever understand what I need to understand,
but in college I told Doc, "Prob'ly by the time
I'm forty   things won't get to me as much."

As I look at my life, I'm afraid   and earlier today,
in the mirror, I saw my mother's face
shocked at how old I am. *My goodness! How old
are you?*
              And when I tell her, she's sure
I'm lying—and to be honest, I just
don't know if I'm the age I am. Each year
part of a conversation   I almost had
with someone I meant to call.

You think maybe all you do adds up
to a definable sum: the eulogy,
a small fire that lets survivors
warm their chilly hands, but really
nobody knows
what turned inside you or why
evolution has guaranteed that
none of us stick around. Last night,

a friend shrugged, "Might as well be positive,"
and I want to believe in people   because I'm a person:

I think about kindness, how it flickers
in a darkened place

and lynching—how some people loved it—
and Malcolm X, his soul sweetened after Mecca,

dying with buckshot scalding his chest,
but whoever mentions Yuri Kochiyama

holding his head in her lap. I believe
in the last light of her hand on his cheek.

Across the street, beneath a sky-blue sky, trees
black-barked and bare. I'm in a café now, surrounded
by clattery laughs and scrambled chatter, a mad jazz
that would scatter birds. What is it
with this world? A while back,

one of my boys died. I heard about it long after—
the funeral, somewhere in Georgia—so in my mind's eye,
Dewey's still *doin the bump*, party-whistle gleaming
in his mouth, "Jungle Boogie" forever *rockin the house.*

I used to think my lucky days made me
different somehow—"some angel
payin my way"—like my mom said
but this poem

could just as easily be Dewey, almost
remembering me   at the same party
under the same groove: my fantastic history
filed down to a few finger-pops and some *Kool*

& The Gang. It's hard to breathe
without the delusion that magnified my life.

I sat across from him in class. We both
wrote poetry. Does everyone secretly

believe they're indispensable? I sit
inside this self   amazed by my face

which is brown and unremarkable.

MAGNIFYING GLASS

No one
would burn
your name
for not seeing
the ant's
careful antennae
testing the air
next to your
shoe, six legs
almost rowing
it along. Who

would be upset
if you brushed one
offhandedly off
your arm, undone
by the tiny
steps: *what do
they want,*
you ask—unaware
that they breathe
through their
sides. Do they
sleep? Do they
dream
anything? No
one should

mark your soul
short   if you
mash one: when
two ants meet
there's no tongue
for hello—it's a
bug, a nearly
less than

little thing: at most,
made to chisel
crumbs
under the fridge
with eyes that
even in brightest
day see not reds
or greens but gray
and gray again.
Who would

curse your life
if you bring out
the *Raid?*
How many books
have they
read?—that
brain   a virtual
speck. Is all
they carry
really work

or just some
dumb old daily
ado?—the heart
spending

what blood, what
prehistoric nudge
on those
handsome,
brittle heads.

ONE TURN AROUND THE SUN

Early day, early summer, liquid sunlight
soaking the city and crape myrtle trees bring back
their pink and purple blooms: how can it happen
again, again—Earth spins and dawn unwraps
the night world as if to say *show me a story*
and the eyes blink

and hearts turn over—something like engines, maybe
like clocks—and not only in beds but in branches—
the chickadees, the quick squirrels, the katydids
and underground the ants: the million-million hum
that one note that makes the grassroots giggle—
and what about this chronic itch, this brimming
sky that asks everything to come on:

the emerald moss, the millipedes, the old
oaks holding their ground—even shade glides
like a cool animal, while people smolder
secretly   as if *self* were a sort of fever,
our heads rising as if we might sail: Monday,
Monday,

then Monday—a month of days,
a month like a cricket   in your hand
then gone. I can't understand
Time   how it makes us and makes us
disappear. I keep turning back
to memory—my life, 59 years spent:
my job, a dead parrot on my shoulder,
bills flocking like flies to the corpse:

what can anybody do? Time
running like ants all over the afternoon
and where are *they* going with so many legs—

as if it made sense to live in a frenzy,
as if their legs had a life of their own
and the little things were getting carried away,
those pepper-speck eyes reading one version

of what daylight brings: Trouble and his
magic hat   what the night almost hides—
the homeless brotha, his missing teeth
a trail of crumbs to the Starbucks
parking lot, "Back in the day, I played guitar,"
he grins—some glint of good music
glossing his face. My shades
muffle the glare: me with my
paper money / him with his
hand open

like the door to a house
already burning   or waiting to burn, ready
to burn for both of us—the dollar bills, a book
of matches—and I see what passes for kindness
may not be kind but some kind of clumsy apology
for the monster that mouths *them that got
shall get*, the Moloch that eats every woman,

every man: some bitten in the womb, some later,
some so gently they don't even feel themselves
slip-slide into the throat   and we all try
to dance to this—the prevailing sound
mistaken for music: the humpty-hump
krunked-up bumping hip-hop could be the cry
of a country going under for the third

time: *everybody put your hands in the air
and wave'em like you jus' don't care*—
cells and phones, twitters—tweets, charged
and recharged, telling   telling each other
what? as the big teeth close around us.

When I was a boy, I would get up early
and go outside—summer coming on
like the smell of cinnamon toast—a little dude
shod in sneaks, primed in shorts, my voice
a piccolo! I remember the red ants
on first patrol   strolling up my shins
with a bold nonchalance, giving me
that cool once-over. I could hear them
muttering all they had to do before dusk—

something like discontent twitching a few
antennae: *Why am I out here with six legs and
no pants? I could live for a year on three strawberries—
fuck the colony!* Even then, my mind threw itself
toward what nobody said: my new brain
filling like a blister, the ruckus inside me,
a carnival come to town.

Early summer, Saturday   free time
soaks the city   and this slow-walking woman—
the rich potion of well-made hips, the accent
of such motion slightly muted beneath
her black shorts and of course, I hear my blood
getting dressed: first swerve of self
toward a better orbit—heat lightning

on the heart's coast—the sexual chance,
the Great Maybe: and what about the brave
shock of first touch, the sumptuous crush
of a kiss, the groove communion—thigh
studying thigh / so much of this displaced
by jobs, by septic religion, ghost-dick capitalism,
television—the anytime friend, bright star

with make-believe light, the come-hither
and scold of this colony called America.

I look at Facebook: the hopeful eyes
peeping from the cyber window, the need
to be *seen*, known; I look

at people in bars,
beer and nachos, cooked beef appearing
then gone—young men, young women,
the unconscious ooze of such
beauty and flies landing
unnoticed, planning a future:

war, wars like hit songs   the torn skin
of the daily scrum—cars restless at red lights,
millipede pedestrians, *kill zones*, the big buildings:
boxes full of work to be done, bosses / drones—
bizzy, the word repeated

until it becomes a city itself—everyone
zigging to the zag: blue collars rub
the sore machines, executives graph the goods,
call the shoppers who catch the scent
with their long snouts.

I see the brown faces,
hard masks trying not to look
surprised   by the undeclared siege:
the Mainstream deftly sicks its dogs,
sends the guns, locks the doors.
Night flares her cloak, the moon
bitten, never whole again—I think
about children   how they

smile when we smile, how we
agree not to say what
we know, not to know
what we know   about growing up:
the calendars gone bad, weeks

dashed to chalk, children
squeezed, their big heads
scored in the vice, gnawed
to the cob

like the rest of us—and all
that's left of me now is my want
for that woman who walks a bass line
so slow even her shadow wants to holler.
She doesn't know how sincerely
I would praise the caramel-chocolate
sea salt of her secret body, how well
I would forget the churches and mosques,
the synagogues, the come-along schools.

Give me the pagan cathedral
of a woman's cunt, the dawn
of her mouth meshed with mine,
the good Goddess giddy in her eyes,
the blood in harmony—what time,
what drink so smooth,
what justice better
than the justice lovers do?

Once, once and *once upon a time*,
they tell me I was born, but
I can't remember the muscular push,
the hands, the clanging light.
According to my mother, it was August
and I cried loud   and *loud*.
Wish I knew where they were,
that class of 1955, the nursery choir
that had me burbling a solo—hour
after hour, all of us blind, our little lungs
changing the air: I look back,

I look back at myself looking back,
but the fact is, one morning I was found
on Earth and strangers learned me their ways—
this noise they call speech   and how to act:
right now, I am *behaving* myself—
check out the baby goat gumming
my brow, the normal shirt, pants zipped,
the mischievous eel penned down—I keep
trying to behave: *Act like you have some sense,*
my father says / *Easier said than done,* I say.

It's all I can do to keep from pissing on tree trunks and storefronts,
marking my turf like a two-legged tomcat, scratching this life
as if I belong: I spend alotta time being polite, but
some people   *should have the shit slapped out of 'em*—
and not only presidents and priests, born-agains
and racist pricks but everyday people

like me   who dress up for the status quo, buy
The Beast a burger, then get a half-hearted dry-hump
and a Frenchless kiss in return—fingering
receipts, checking my watch   when I should soak my heart
in kerosene, strike my head like a match! How many
seasons have I nixed for a job? How much craving
tazed in my trousers, while all summer

America becomes *The Land of Tiny Shorts*:

such visibility!—oh me, oh my—
as if I had never before, as if every photon
had flown to teach me light: the swarm swarming
even now: what can I do?—my life, *my life!*
eats my life—already 59 years gone

and some of my friends
gone to ground or gone gah-gah
for *God*   which is worse:
the voluntary blindness—

to chew the same verses
over and over
with the grim donkey—
as if the Earth were not
a hummingbird, as if staying
awake   weren't scripture enough.

Woke up in my wrecked apartment—
a stack of bills, piles of books, fucked-up floors,
stuffed-up nose—couldn't talk
myself out of bed: my coffled heart,
my face stained and washed again—
again until I look like a man trying
to look like a man, but I'm here—*here*
this minute   finding myself
snared in the threads. Have you
ever seen that? A bug moving, then
the sticky tug of what had been
invisible: the mean realization—the sudden

uh-oh knowing exactly what's what:
Death   its bizzy legs   closing in
to tie you up. When I was a boy I threw ants
into webs and watched / didn't know
it was a preview of my life: *believing*,
believing what I saw, what I'd been
told to see   and everywhere

the slaughterhouses wearing
their golden arches, the soldiers
declared necessary, the mantra, *pay more
and save*—the matrix, the tortured
script   disguised as fun, disguised
as your *career*, disguised as a "brand
new car," as credit, as marriage,
as the nuclear family, as Christmas,
as *a day off*, so you can catch up—

the outcome already unmistakable: this
is why the mad go mad, why
the riots and revolutions come back:

this story, this tall tale of brighter
whites and bigger blacks, them prisons
for profit, that football fantasy, this
corporate democracy, these techno
cronies—us bizzy monkeys, we
monkeys online, all them monkeys
on TV—this story is not

our story: to live for *that green,*
to be all about them shiny things
is to be chummed   and gaffed—
is to wake up with a barcode
for a face, to know dawn   as a soldier
sent by the clocks—a prod, a shove,
a hangman petting the scaffold.

Dawn   I knew it once:

peach light, new sky, liquid summer swimming
the breeze the way Her mouth brushes your ear.
Dawn's kiss on the thigh of my soul! My eyes—
two loons, twin musketeers, ten orgasms,
twice kings—revoking the governments and their
armies, rescinding the weekdays and the legions
dying for coffee, dying inch by inch
in the quicksand, in the *getting to work.*

Suppose, just once, you saw a middle-aged maniac
skating telephone wires like a squirrel, or one
glad woman jumping balconies and boulevards
as if time were a trampoline—think how gladly
you would lose your mind: look
what the *Takers* have taken and the monsters

they have made, the tame zombie-playmates
they have made of us: smiling, bobbing
for the job, trotting along when we might be trolls
under their bridges—billy goats butting their
smug asses—when we might rewrite the world!

What is that restlessness? What is this rage?
Proof that the rose still burns in your blood—
root and branch, thorn and bloom, proof
that your brain is a bucking horse, that
your soul remembers and bites the leash; I want
such teeth in *my* mouth. Why can't we
have a world worthy of the wheeling sun?
The Earth is a house that flies!

Fuck all the powers that be.

I remember my parents—my mother
trilling her soprano, my serious father
and his black fists, how they kept on
despite the heavy sleet strafing
their lives: they should be famous
for getting dressed   the morning after
Martin Luther King was killed: I was thirteen,
puberty coming on like a seizure—

I went to the kitchen. My cereal sat there, sugar
snowing on the brown flakes, my mother tilting
the spoon, my father with his Cherokee eyes, cup
rising to his lips, getting ready for the day, getting
ready   no matter what, doing the *had to be done.*
I can't recall what they said, but they were calm—

my brother stabbed his eggs. There would be
riots at Germantown High—and my parents went
to work surrounded by white people who measured
their words /
            I sit here with these pencils meaning

to make some sign, some song, something
like the love I've been given. I feel the pulse
pecking my wrists, but I don't know:

I don't know:

Early sunlight, broken summer, buttery day
the dawn brims over—crape myrtles and cars,
the city birds call to each other, all the people
simmering 98.6 degrees, this blood
shuffled with history, the DNA

whispering *persist! persist!* Every heart
a political prisoner, every one of us force-fed
some version of what the daytime brings,
what the midnight hides. Already Death
sketches my face, my beard drawn gray.

Century after century, He opens
his scabby arms, while rise upon rise,
little kids rush the land, tasting the details,
meaning to take it all back, believing themselves
the first, the smartest, the true: *back in the day*,
I *was*   a child—and everything was a soft cookie!

But the members of the Klan were babies once
and the officers of the Third Reich too and the killers
called Janjaweed   and Dick Cheney and his puppet,
The Idiot, and Tojo and the Taliban
and Assad and Mugabe and everyone
who swung a blade in Rwanda, and
the rapists running the rape camps—
and the chemists who chemmed napalm
and the Khmer Rouge, and all the slave
masters with their bizzy cocks and every
gun-gaming cop and the man who shot
Mahatma Gandhi: every one   a child once,

coming from the rainforest warmth
of a woman's womb, every one
taught the amnesia—like me:
I was the goofy boy

pressed into knickers and knee socks—
my mother tucked a napkin under my chin,
made gingerbread with blackstrap molasses,
read me *The Billy Goats Gruff, Little Black
Sambo, A Child's Garden of Verses*—how I grew
beneath the sky of her voice, how ready to run:

> *Eenie-meenie-mynie-moe*
> *Catch a doggie by the toe*
> *If he hollers let him go*—

I hid and chased, flew and fell—was wings
and no bird, my legs spinning
as if they had a life of their own.

I spend adulthood trying to blend in, trying
not to be the stranger who's become strange—
trying not to be IT: that lost brotha
in the parking lot trying to sing,
smelling like moldy piss and dead dog
with no lovers or friends, with no place
to sleep   though sleep has become harder

and harder to find / O friends! The sun comes back
again, again—only to find us strumming our
dim teeth, filling our pants, sucking the workday's
mangy tit, while the ants, the trillion-trillion

hum just beneath us: do you think
they think   we *know* something? I've held a few,
felt the ready bite of those tiny jaws. Imagine
your own self grabbed

by something ten thousand times your size
and deciding to bite it! To be in the clutch
of a monster and still sink your whole life
into one stupefying chomp meaning *get off me
goddammit!* Isn't that what courage is for?—
to lay claim to your life, to roam beyond the grasp,
beyond the rule of whoever means to use you as fuel

for bad machinery. Break open your eyes!
the night—without being asked, with no vote
and no compromise—backs off for the sun.
The days are more than we say they are: dawn
gives birth to them all, names none—
the minutes riot, time flames in every direction.

Let's get out of this, this

stupor called *a normal day*, this dumb farm
called *country* / We starve
with the feast nearby and we swallow
the words of a story nobody wants to tell
but why? Why be practical?—when The Hour
rips Her gown, kicks down your door

and wraps Her big legs around you—why pretend
you *don't* know what I mean?
                                          Yesterday,
after thrashing a *Tastykake Krimpet*,
I saw an ant stealing a crumb way, way
bigger than possible—I was downtown:

Chevys flexed their engines, pedestrians pushed on—
sandals, high heels, sneaks, bizness kicks—some mouths
smoking, some spending talk through a small box,
trying for the ear of someone invisible, someone
who makes the daily knock hurt less.

I believe it is hard to be human, to be these
new animals, hard to say yes to this singular
blood   and to the flying world that made us:
Who keeps conjuring the Distractions? Who?

Who? What are the Words that gnaw on the soul?

Our heads smolder and blaze, slow light
gaining the streets—maybe now,

maybe now   it is time
to be born:

early day, open summer, a slight breeze
over the sleepers, our tired legs

on edge—we circle the sun
in so many ways: *this* Earth

and all the other planets
holding their own.

THIRTY-THIRTY BLUES VILLANELLE

Who can tell a man not to go where he goes?
I laid the long tracks; my life waves from the train
I was thirty almost thirty years ago

Being grown up means you're s'posed to know
Although I don't know what I can explain—
And I was thirty   like thirty years ago

I bend with the music breaking hard but slow
Jobs kidnap the daylight, then leave the remains:
"Just kiss me goodbye when it's time to go"

It looks like we're losin' but say it ain't so:
Dumb news and new killers get most'a the fame
Why tell a man not to run when he goes?

My dad's on a walker, his whole life in tow
If you'd seen him at forty, you'd say *what a shame*
But he was forty almost fifty years ago

Sanity works hard to put on the good show
But still some fine folks go off in the brain
They couldn't know   that they didn't know

Why needle a riddle when the answer is No?
Been poking the troubles, but the Trouble remains
And I've been thirty since thirty years ago

I look at young men and think *where did I go?*
Play some guitar while Death tunes my name

Guess this is the *what*   I should already know
'Cause I was thirty thirty years ago

MORNING WHERE YOU ARE

Don't go around looking like I would
if I could, but if I can how can I?
                                    —Mom

Some spring days
she and her sister, Eva,
strolled up Boyer Street
and you could tell

they were *The Bluford Girls*
again—blue suits, black heels,
gold pins—and early April
pulled up in its cool limousine.

I was a teenager then
and had no idea what
that walk meant: the royalty
in it, the defiance—how

in what seemed a few years,

what could never end
would end: my aunt dies
on a bad mattress,
one flat soda in the fridge

and my mother, stolen
from herself, her smile
no longer made
for her mouth.

————

Maybe now   it's always sunlight
splintered behind the trees: evening,
the wind down. Cars

like conversations, pause
and move on—my mind walking
its three-legged dog

from this   to that
and once more, I begin
to think about Barbara Bluford,

English teacher, pinochle player
born on a train bound for Virginia:

my mother grew up a city girl,
proud of her father, the one
black dental surgeon in Philadelphia.

When I was little, I'd sit on her lap
and wave from the window: *my* father
waving back, headed for the bus.

It was the early '60s: the news
just beginning to bleed.

She was kind and solid in that
take-no-nonsense parental way
and dressed so sharp

that a glimpse might cut'cha.
Those hats she wore to church:
bronze feathers blazing against gold

or the rose crown with the cream band
braided around a brim so wide
it held another sky.

*

Some nights we played Pokeno.
Four glasses, grape *Kool-Aid*:

me, my brother, and my Dad.
She filleted the cards
like a 5-star chef.

The kitchen clock adding up,
the tiny jackpot ripening.

                    *

My mother swears she's never cooked
a turkey; though for five decades
she did it twice a year. Last Wednesday
she started pouring *Wheaties*
at sunset. I was on the phone:

"It's evening, ma—*evening*."
She said, "It may not be morning

where *you* are, but it's
morning *here*."

Before the bad dentures,
she had the gladdest smile—

a morning unto itself:
any day starting over
wherever she found us.

"In college,"
my father said,
"she used to smile
like that   *at me*."
_____

When she slipped in the lecture hall
he picked her up—Fisk University,
September 1945:

WWII barely over, fallout still flying the stratosphere.
Lamplit nights, my father below her window,
his Kappas to her Deltas—the brothers in chorus,
his hopeful solo climbing the ivy   *Only you...*

*

Picture the lit major
in Arna Bontemps' English class: her midcalf skirt,
her blouse, blue jay blue, the matching pumps,
hand up, the answer a lantern in her eyes—

and Mr. Chemistry, *Thomas Seibles, III*—
dapper cat from Oklahoma, snap-brim hat,
pinstripe suit, spit-shined shoes, that easy
side-to-side shuttle of his shoulders when he walked:

*

my nearly adult parents, beautiful—
their bodies still brand new.
On their honeymoon, Niagara Falls
must've flashed over them like an avalanche:

a passion like sunrise that first time,
like meeting a Prophet and having all
the answers asked.

————

Growing up, I thought
I knew what   was what,
the hammer of each day

barely missing me, *me*
with my mother's face,
my father's heavy hands—

so this is what
what turns into: bits
of your life straggling
behind you—empty cans
hitched to the newlyweds' car

or the ragged tail of one red kite,
my father playing it
like a big fish in the sky,

and my mother
brushing my *Brillo* head,
teaching me the wonderful
"cinnamon toast" and how
to act in church

and not to wear polka dots
with plaids.

MOSAIC

> *I'm a'kickin' but not high,*
> *and I'm a'flappin' but I can't fly*
> —Florence Church

A carpet of light, the
ocean alive < half a moon
muting the stars.

I tell myself
despair   is just

a bad attitude: *Get up,*
I say. *Look—*
and the shimmer

spends its name
in my head.

———

These days   midlife
holds the jagged edge:

my nephew in prison,
a *prisoner* > friends insane

with work or sick
of trying to be loved,

my parents handing over their lives
like evidence: my good mother,

her mind   a trail of crumbs
in a woods flocked with birds.

--/--

To *raise* a child   break it
like a wild horse—
bend the will: *get up,*
get dressed.

I remember Emlen School
staring me down, my lunch box,
September:
the spiked fence freshly painted.

Then, the goodbye from my mother
who'd fought my hard hair,
lipstick like mist on my cheek.

--/--

That instant when eyes meet
and slide away—even love
blinks, looks off

like a stranger.

With: Who are you
with?

--/--

I suspect   *everything.*

Outside the air moves
a giant bird I cannot see.

Still laced in this
brown body, my aging heart:
kah-doom   kah-doom-doom
still minds my thoughts

but rolls his eyes.

———

To see > < to be seen: the life
of the visible. Don't be shy.

Glances pick my face.

Once, I was a sperm and an egg
but you didn't see me.

          --/--

Too small to walk
alone: I held

my father's index
finger. Philadelphia police

caped in their black
jackets, big badges   almost

hungry   looking at us.

          --/--

In a mall—say a *food court*
on Saturday   or a stadium
just before the game.

There's this drone, this
steady, muttering thrum

punctured by
packages—plastic this,
paper that—torn and torn.

"It's hard not to be hungry."

          --/--

242

Time   for bed: my
mother reading *The
Three Little Pigs*, doing
all the voices. Remember
the pictures—those piggy
pants and shirts?

--/--

When you   *see me*,
what is that

image in the eye?
Solid ghosts, we are pictured
here—in the lit world.

Visible: we *want* to be seen: skin,
fancy legs   shoes and hats.

To want > to be seen and
wanted. Nice lips with a moist

sheen. Eyes, like mouths.
_____

What tortures, what tortures
me is   the question: *what*
are other people   thinking?

I keep watch—a vast horde
of Nikes has landed, running
sea   to shining sea.

--/--

In America skin was
where you belonged, a who

you were   *with*, a reason

someone might: how—*at the*

parties   of hands unknown—

astonishing deaths
could meet you.

———

Reckless eyeballs.

Three centuries track me,
their dumb dogs slobbering
on my scent: Myself runs

into my   other self: *Over here!*

my self whispers—*Freedom*

over here!

        --/--

Six years old, I sang
like a chickadee. My father

slapped me for handing him
the scissors

wrong. What did I know?
What did I know?

        --/--

Suppose nobody knows
what's

inside you.
But you, yourself,
find it pretty clear:

anxiety   adding up, leveling off,
doubling > some comfort in people
you think you
understand / frustration,

fatigue, a secret.
One worn constellation
marking the lusciousness of sex.

     --/--

What's your faith? Which skin
do you believe? The *unseen*

stays with us:
the air

rubbing your lungs
right now—

nations of germs
feuding over your hands.

     --/--

Savory sweet salt of sweat in summer,
a taste of almonds, some buttery bread.

The loins, a house of hunger, personal
but not personal: the way moonlight calls

for you and   not for you. What
I want > I guess < *I want.*

Fingernails grow. My
belly grumbles. My blood runs

up a long hill.
_____

Among *the brothaz*, a certain
grip   in the eyes. A sense

of something
swallowed   not chewed—

as if they'd been made
a story and were dying

to untell themselves:
profiles—prisons,

the sports inside The Sport.
Outside, the wolf

with a
huff   and a puff.

       --/--

Culture: a kind of knife:
cuts one way   opens
your brain to a certain
breed of light   shaves
consciousness to its

purpose, its cross: the nail
thru your hand > < your
other hand holding
the hammer.

       --/--

Once, I asked my father
if he knew   *everything.*

I was hopeful, seven—
a corn muffin
where my head shoulda been.

I saw him shave and after,
little dabs of Kleenex on the nicks.

--/--

I only see
The Game   in pieces—
the rules inside me
like bad wiring < like a shadow
government < like dark
matter in a sky
otherwise Mardi Gras'ed
with stars. Rise up,
somebody   somebody

--/--

(Insert your life here.)

--/--

Did you mean to be this way?
Did you mean to become
something you didn't mean?

You didn' become
something you   didn'
mean   did you?

--/--

Image follows image, quack follows
quack—a line of lonely ducks. What

is wrong   is well

organized: see all the schedules
with their *Coors Lights* and comfy socks.
_____

How do I look? With whom > < am I with?

Better worlds build hives
inside us. Last words

trapped like wasps in our mouths.

     --/--

So monogamy   never made
sense to me, nor most of what
was called *growing up*.

The whole
haunted house

of race and religion   of sex,
money, possession.

Am I rented or owned?
How many lives turned
on the spit? How many
hours _____
and _____?

     --/--

I was nine, integrating Anna
Blakiston Day School: fourth grade,

248

mixing it up. Visible,

with my new face.
Whenever my mother
had to see my teachers

she'd say,
"Don't send me into battle

with a butter knife."

--/--

Connect this to that, *this*
to that: word   by word, a
sentence

scavenges the alleys
like a lost pet—fur matted,
leg cut: the hunger,

a sort of riddle > his noise
some sort of answer.

———

What skinny faith you have—
and such big teeth: *all*

the better. I mean to step out
of history   for just a minute

to feel my blood float

above the *say-so.* Memory,
a jar of flies. Spin off the lid.

I forget what you know. What

did you *ever* know?

--/--

To speak: score the alphabet—
make the shape of what

cannot be seen. Tear it open

like a child with a new bag
of something / stand in the traffic

goading your throat until the song
sharpens in your mouth—

the solo: one nick
chasing another.

--/--

I think I'm
starting to know
Everything < O, tongue!
O, summer! O, bold
bare legs of women
upon which my soul beads
like sweat > O, rosemary rolls
and marmalade!
Hard-bodied beetles
with your six-legged sashay!
O,
funky beats and bitter
guitars < O, children
taller and taller no
matter
what!

O, moonlit sea! O, Hershey bars!
O, bizness besuited

pigeons of death: *How   much
does   it   cost?*

———

One dandelion head gone to seed,
half-flung on the wind.

I've sold a lot of myself already:
already alotta my selves been sold.

I have this feeling

every day—*something* I know
that can't

be words. This life
stuffs my eyes.

These people nearby—syllables

like pheasants flushed
from their mouths.

I'm back on my mother's lap
waving my small arms.

WITH NO HAT: NEW POEMS (2017–2020)

I have a hummin' bird that can hum so loud
You'd think you were losin' your mind

—Jimi Hendrix

IT HAD BEEN A LONG TIME

since the poem had seen a sunset: trees, tall buildings

black against the burnt-orange sky. The breeze soft, like—
like a sigh for a friend long dead.

Nothing to do now but try to stay clean.
And think. The poem never

tells anyone   it had been "incarcerated"

which sounds like a way to cook meat.

Afraid, always kind of. Impossible not to remember
certain faces   the hard quiet of men

Even out here:
this light

the feeling of being trapped—
as if a country   could itself be a cage.

Something invisible: an idea, a germ, something
had worked on everybody.

Night now. The poem
looks back at the city,

sees the moon   not up, two headlights
shivving the dark.

THE DEAD PLAY BLUES VILLANELLE

Feels like I'm awake, but I can't really tell
I think I'm alive, but I'm not really sure
Do the dead ever try to remember themselves?

High-Def is so clear, there's almost a smell
I'm grillin a burger and cheering the scores
I think I'm awake, but I can't ever tell

When they want you to buy it, they know it'll sell
They just seed your head with a digital spore
That's why the dead shop amongst themselves

The Dark holds a flush and I see His tell
But play my bad hand like a pestering sore
No reason to fold when you're under the spell

If that isn't water   what'chu think's in the well?
Gravediggers stay bizzy, but who's keeping score?
When I'm dead will I still wanna talk to myself?

You know what *I* know, but let's never tell
We'll shuffle along trailing blood on the floor
And pretend to be *woke* while we're under the spell

Maybe I just need to pinch myself
Would love to get out, but they left out the door
I think I'm awake, but you never can tell

I'd rather go live with the radical elves
I don't even look at the news anymore

But I turn on the game 'cause I'm under the spell
And eat while the dead play amongst themselves

THE DOLLARS

"I'm all in"

Do they own you?
Do they
make you
do whatever
they want? Do they

own you? Do you
work and pay and
work? Are you
nervous?

Is it hard
to sleep? Do they
got you? Was it
hard to wake
up?

What about your *hair*?
Does it keep
happening? Are you
doing your
best?
Do you need
a little
something?

Are you dressed?
Are you getting dressed?
Are you almost dressed?
What about
your hair?

Are you tired? Are you
hard to wake up?

What time is it?
How about
now? Do they
need more? Do they
make you? Did they
make you

over? Are you half-
dressed? Do they
own you? Do you
think
what you're
supposed to? Are you
saving? Who
are you

saving? Are you

nervous? Are they
watching? Is it
hard?
Do you *ever*
wake up?
Do they
own you? Do you
wake up

when they
want you to? Are they
everywhere? Are you
on
time?

How about now?
How about

now? Do you
do *the work*? Did you do

the do? Did they
do you?

Are you trying
to get
dressed?
Are you? Did you?
Will you?

Do they
own you?
Do they *still*
own you?

AMUSEMENT PARK

Shuffling along, shouldering softly through the crowd,
you don't remember the admission or planning

to come. The rides look new, but it's mostly
the paint. Every day the sun disappears

and reappears   as if unsure of the situation.
Your parents used to talk about being

"young once." Now, you wonder what they
really wanted to say. Shadows

scratch the sidewalk. Popcorn, hot dogs,
pizza: aromas stoke the breeze.

Of course, fear takes the air too—
like the kind of perfume you only notice

when it's gone. You told your friends
"I'm sick of this shit," but somehow,

here you are   back in line,
itching for the Wicked Flea, a ride

famous for jumping the tracks, but
the whole park is like that. Even

the cross-eyed calico creeps
low to the ground as if ready

for some bad surprise. Worrying
this way, the cat is a lot like

the people who come here
to undo their daily lives: built

on hard work and
and scary news—and bigotry,

which usually moves around disguised
as someone else. Wherever you turn,

women, men: almost every hue, some skin
so dark it holds a hint of stars, other faces

white as paper, cinnamon-gold, cocoa
with a kiss of brass. Of course, the fear

is shared unevenly—with all these colors
and the history they recall—but the people

remain lovely, enticing—a smorgasbord ready
to be consumed   and, though strangers

exchange harmless glances, each
suspects the rest of playing a part

in a story that seems impossible
to explain—like the park itself:

both natural and not, both
deadly and full of fun.

The Crazy Crook is the scariest: *guaranteed
to remix your mind*, the neon winks. Some get on

with glee, some with stolid faith, but you go
half-doubting, half-hoping it'll be alright

like your parents said   though lately, you haven't
seen them on any rides. Its height is legendary,

the loop-d-loops ridiculous. Your friends believe
it's the one ticket worth fighting for: that long, first

climb, the haphazard twists and dives, the whoops,
the shrieks   and every time somebody yelling,

"Look, ma, no hands!" Maybe the loudmouth
is a superhero—ready to pretend

the courage that might make
Death and his shiny badge

back off—or maybe he's just another dumb chump
begging to be noticed in a world that

repaints and forgets, refuels and drives on.
"Sit your simple ass down!" you snap,

while the Crazy Crook rolls over those bone-
bending swerves that snatch the riders

back to their bizzy, befuddled, stampeded lives:
out of hand and harder, faster—

as if some cranked-up kidnapper has everyone
locked in his trunk and won't stop

stomping the gas: the days blur, each month
honks by like a V of Canada geese—you

spin around: your friends keep testing their
new knees. How did you get used

to this? When did you forget
how to sleep? What

made your parents
play certain words over

and over—*job, success,
love, responsibility*—and where,

exactly where did they go?

SEEKING ASYLUM,

the poem enters quietly—
without any state-approved
ID, with nothing that says
where it belongs. Many things
had become unbearable, so
much so that, when
the official asks *Why*
did you

leave your country,
the poem turns
its palms up and sobs
at the shiny white vinyl walls
until two uniforms haul it
out the door, down the hall,
bruised into the bustling
lunchtime street

where the blur of pedestrians,
every few steps, is punctuated
by homeless persons—some
screaming as if to disprove
their invisibility, some curled
like commas on the sidewalk.
A wind pats down the trees:
heavy clouds have come
uninvited, crowding the city
sky. *Maybe I can't belong*

anywhere,
the poem mutters, so
no one will hear. *Maybe*
I shoulda said
I had to leave 'cause
there's nowhere left to go, though

the poem—who'd spent its life
trying to be clear—knew
those words
didn't make any sense.

Being itself a stranger
estranged, the poem is bugged
by a niggling question
about its own true
origins. *But Who Really
Gives A Shit?!* the poem shouts
as the back-to-work citizens
veer and scatter.

In some shop windows
the poem almost sees its face:
brown, indelible, familiar,
disappearing quietly
like the mist that had just
begun to fall.

LITTLE STAR BLUES VILLANELLE

Someday no one will wonder where you are
Your name won't be on anyone's mind
Remember "Twinkle, Twinkle, Little Star"?

Count up the hours you scratched in your car
Where were you going most of the time?
Someday no one will wonder where you are—

Maybe you think I take things too far
I think it was mom who taught me to rhyme
She sang *Twinkle, twinkle, little star*

Some days die like big bugs in the tar
Who was that small boy at the start of your mind?
Someday your mother won't know who you are

Woulda been nice to be crowned the czar
Tell everyone else what to do all the time:
You betta twinkle, twinkle, little star!

Whatchu think makes people work so hard?
Like money's some mountain we s'posed to climb
One day no one will wonder how you are

Mostly what kills me won't leave any scar
I bet I know why most people go blind
They need "Twinkle, Twinkle, Little Star"

Let's sit in the shade by that tree in the yard
And chew on the hours with their lemony rind

Someday no one will wonder what you are
Remember "Twinkle, Twinkle, Little Star"

POEM AT 64

for Michael Ryan

Always surprised to be
the age I am, though I guess
everything since puberty, I remember—
that first wet dream, leaving home
for college, *Shaft in Africa*,
scooping ice cream at Swenson's—

and I am by now, by all appearances,
someone who has *succeeded* somehow,
while a few good friends and early loves
have left this life, passed away,
"gone on," like my dad would quip
and shrug. What to do about so much

vanishing: the lazy grin you won't see
jump to a laugh, that voicemail
you cannot answer—
and finding your own jolly self
in line for departure, not wanting
to go but traipsing to the exit

anyway—like drifting toward the door
near the end of a party: chatting
with her and him, hugging some,
squeezing hands, and then
you're completely outside:
streetlights and shadowy trees

walking you to the car. It just
doesn't matter maybe—maybe
it just   doesn't matter
what we think about death,
that grief
is harder than anything

anyone can do. My father,
with his love for Count Basie
and lumpy buttermilk, is now
ashes. He has *gone on*,
joined The Chapter Invisible
as his Kappa brothers would say.

I remember him at 64—
forking sardines from those flat cans,
some nights pretending to be Redd Foxx,
then trudging up the stairs like
any other unfamous man. This was
twenty-five years before he found himself

staring down *The Rifleman* on TV,
almost nonchalantly waiting
for his diaper change. No one ever
imagines: I don't imagine
ever   struggling with a fork, hoping
someone will come to feed me.

My mother, slow-strolling the
Alzheimer's Road, still doesn't know
she's a widow. One time
she asked about "that man
who used to be here" the way
you'd inquire about a friend

not seen since high school
or an ice cream shop
closed long ago. I'm not mad

at anybody. Got nobody
to blame   though a bad
feeling keeps pushing me

around   like Big Sid used to
back in seventh grade.
Today I'm 64: born

sixty-four years ago,
today. And I might be here again
next year, but right now—

if I could make the time
and make myself less afraid—

I would cry like a baby
for everyone.

MY MOTHER

May 1, 2020 / 5:38 P.M.

This is what I remember:

Between her two last breaths
a long hesitation—

as if she thought she'd
heard something and paused

hoping it might be repeated
or maybe she finally realized

what she'd wanted to say all
along   and was not dying

just holding out for the words
so she could explain

something funny and unfortunate
and absolutely true

like on the phone with Auntie Margie
years ago: the story of a friend's

hard kiss that cracked a man's
front tooth. "Yes indeedy," she'd say

after a long, eye-watering laugh—
Yes indeedy.

Earlier, close to noon,
her eyes had opened

and she seemed to see
what we did not   but managed

only a noise, an inflection
probably older than this hovering

shadow called language. I admit
I *did* think that she had always

and only been *my mother*—so
it's true, I did not know her

as well as I like to pretend
which doesn't make me

much more than just a little
lost   like most of us when we

really think about our mothers:

how they lived, who they were
before we came along.

She didn't open her eyes again
or acknowledge in any way

that you and I were sitting there
afraid, not knowing when the last

would come—as if death itself had been
detoured, traveling slow back roads

from far away. Hard to tell
if she could still hear us

or if our hands on her arm
were comfort or nuisance

or if she had already set out
for another place

where remembering exactly
and trying to explain

doesn't matter at all.

EITHER WAY

for Cornelius Eady

Days when something grazes my shoulder.

Sunlight, sidewalk, the shadows sharp.

The sky holds a cold, unbreakable blue
that says *Why look   up here?*

*

Doesn't seem like so far back: couldn't dance,
scared of girls, I heard Smokey sing

goin to a go-go   with that soft crystal in his voice.
Pictures, music caught somewhere in my head—

I'm sick of memory:

my younger self, still inside,
wanting a way out of this

who I am now: this bizzy-all-the-time,
this—this itch middle of my back.

*

But who was that kid in the basement?—

all alone with *The Miracles*
moving his feet. The orange couch

covered in plastic, black marks
on the beige linoleum.

*

Something about solitude—if you can stand it—
makes you feel wise: the voice

in your head   talking its way somewhere,

pressing you to believe
what it says

and, though you can't remember when,
you grow into it

or you don't: each thought breaks
into the next—keeps on, turns back.

Either way, you don't ever
really   under

                    *

stand. Just as you get used to the snow
shingling your hair, your idols, one

by one, begin to leave. Their old tunes
fill the coffee shops

and gently bob your head.
What is it

                    *

that your life
forgot to mention?

Hum a few bars you say.

WITH NO HAT,

no shirt, no pants, the poem walks
the early afternoon. Summer sun
spots the odd shape on the road
and offers a cloud for shade.

The poem is headed downtown
with its revelations, its beauty, all
the intricate parts finally
open to the general public

who, though they try to deny it,
have always wanted to see
beneath the vintage clothes.
The poem's previous modesty

and stealth, its humility and
restraint, its patient, soft-spoken
invitations have served no one really—
not even the poem itself, which has
always wanted the spotlight:

the red carpet, the sequined gown,
the top hat, velvet lapels, ruby
slippers, all its big, front teeth
inlaid with gold. The first people
the poem passes look   look away

look again: their hope swelling
like a fresh bump on the head.
One guy tries *9-1-1*, but the 9
skips then shimmies like a new

disciple, and the brotha's big 'fro
bursts into cotton candy. The poem
loves it, loves being out, being *seen*—
the almost-cool walk flips

to a Denzel stroll: *I'm kickin new
flava in ya ear,* it says unquietly,
meeting the eyes of drivers who swerve,
so sure they see what must be

a mirage: a buck-naked angel
rump-shakin beside the witless
sprawl of their lives, their heads
anointed with apocryphal music.
The cars refuse the road—

their horns reborn scatting
a fanfare of *Funkadelic* clarinets.
This is my body, the poem says.
Take and eat.

COME HOME, LADY

for Madam Daylight

Without you, the seconds limp
like sad millipedes
in hard shoes. Minutes sag
like bad lectures
in the late afternoon. Like old men
out of smokes, the hours
itch and fidget
but soon

your smile—that shard of shooting star,
that softly candling chandelier
will take my room. Your hips
slick wheels for a hot race!
When I see you, my soul
is a sous chef—my heart

rubs itself a zest
worthy of your mouth.
Your kiss: April clarinet
for this grim November, big
Orange Crush for my
dust-bunny life.

O, let me be that one
come-hither morsel, that
savory flavor and shine
on your lips: what's sorrow
but a grown man
stuffed in the trunk
of his worry?

Your legs! Lady,
your legs—long as an Alaskan
summer day! That easy gait:

your velvet thighs, your deeply
wise and wicked ways—

when I see you
we will dance like bumper cars
on rubber streets, like lazy ducks
on crazy lakes, like hippos and hobos
in toe-shoes!

SOMETIMES FREDDY BLUES VILLANELLE

for Freddy Porter

Sometimes Freddy   would talk to the trees
And the brothaz would just laugh half the time
But a few of 'em said *Have mercy on me*

Think about all that good sunlight you see
Yet somehow the days peel away like rind
Mostly Freddy just talked to the trees

Branches say somethin when they shake in the breeze
Believe what'chu want, but it could be a sign
Maybe they're sayin *Have mercy on me*

Sundays I sit with a brain full'a fleas
And listen to people speak for the Divine
Wish they would go and just talk to the trees

Hiding a scream is like holdin a sneeze
It's all you can do not to lose your damn mind
I see why people say *Have mercy on me*

I'm starting to list like a ship in rough seas
I guess you just have to laugh half the time
And think about Freddy and walk with the trees

I look at my watch, but my watch is a tease
Or maybe it's always a quarter past nine
Them thin little hands have mercy on me

Think about SpongeBob with his home in the sea
Wouldn't you visit if you had the time?

Sometimes Freddy   would talk to the trees
You can see why I say *Mercy, mercy on me*

GAME DAY

for Colin Kaepernick

Here they come: Bobbleheads.
Hot dogs. Big dudes and beer.

The stadium, a living thing.
Little kids fizz like fresh *Pepsi*.

You always loved the game.
Didn't you always get picked first

in the schoolyard: like stepping
into a good dream—the ball

in your hands, you were a snake
with wings: a shimmy, a shake

and the defense disappeared.

Then came your faith
in highlights—catch,

cutback, touchdown, blood—

the stars pointing up
to a God they knew kept score

and the cheerleaders: sequins
in their eyes, smiles you hoped

meant something sexual. The TV
sizzled and blazed, and the players

on your posters promised
someday you might never be alone:

crossing a street, cruising the mall,
your face, the big surprise—your long run,

the ESPN on everyone's lips.
You had to believe

a bright jersey and a good arm
could change everything,

even your tough country.

And weren't they wonderful,
those days when you knew nothing

could catch you—*runnin*
like he was late for the last bus!—

and maybe what gave you that
sidestep, that blind speed

was partly fear: The Past

reset, always scheming
to chase you down.

But wasn't the NFL *The Emerald City?*

Weren't you the flying house?
for awhile. Weren't you

Dorothy? Weren't you

the Scarecrow
and the Wizard of Oz?

Hard for anyone to believe
that History is no dream.

The stadium rings, even now
like a medieval cathedral:

the anthem fades, the uneasy
citizens take their seats.

These days, you watch it all
on TV. You remember

bright mustard, fresh
meat boosting the breeze—

and when one team starts to lose,
the shouts and jeers replay

some old questions: *who's bleeding
on the field? Who's howling*

from the stands? How simply
this long season continues—

like a kind of obedience,
a bone bruise that lingers

or some other thing
not mentioned in the song:

MAGA HAT III: STRATEGY

You plant seeds so something will grow.
At some point, you want your plate full, right?
You have to anticipate, *plan ahead*—

you think pride is different than corn?
You reap what you sow like The Bible says.
Once upon a time, we owned everything,

even basketball, but we got fat, got soft: *equality.*
Now, you have miscegenation everywhere.
Just think about that.

If you fear winter don't wait till December
to start chopping wood. And there's been a cold front
since the '60s, since the hippies and Dr. Koon.

But springtime is coming: feel that balmy breeze?
Look after where you live. *See about it and
be about it,* I always say. What we've planted

will decide how we'll eat—just like yesterday
grew from all the yesterdays preceding. You don't
really think American history happened

by accident—as if the forefathers didn't mean
to do what they did. *They meant it* and they meant
for us to follow their lead. Did they *ever*

mention *diversity?* To say it simply:
some lives matter more.
Remember

who *does* and who *don't.* Good people
weren't unhappy—until the Civil War:
Them good ol' days are calling like morning birds.

Liberals and mud people see Trump and wonder
how *that* got inside the White House.
They've got no sense

of the long-term, the work required
to bring the harvest. *The Donald* is a seed.
They think today   started this morning.

NOT NEARLY ENOUGH

for César Vallejo

Yesterday, maybe—tomorrow perhaps
but *today*, no one is reading
my poems, no one at all!
It's as if my whole life
has been covered like a parrot's cage
so everybody can get some sleep.

I didn't mean to shout, to blaspheme,
to interrupt, curse, use slang, obsess
over women's thighs. I did not
mean to cause trouble—did I?
Maybe I did. Of course, I did

but for the best possible reasons:
1.   There's no pretty way to fight ugliness.
2.   There's not nearly enough love going around,
3.   nowhere near an adequate array of sexual
4.   collaborations: in fact, a wild lack
5.   of empathy and daring, especially
6.   from God who has fallen disastrously
7.   short of my expectations.

Where is the man who sees war on TV
and runs screaming naked down the street
with the head of his johnson flapping
back and forth, thigh to thigh
like a flag in a jockless wind!?

And, with her marvelously chocolate booberoos
glossed with sunlight and saliva, where is
the woman who bursts into Our Lady of Hope
Cathedral singing *Tell me somethin good*!?

We see children, we *were* children—
with dolls that peed, with wooden trucks

and wind-up frogs and hide & seek—
who knew better than what our parents said.

Tell me: how did we let these fuckheads run the world
off the road?! We cannot tuck our brains
up our asses then wonder why self-sucking morons
come to power—with their sad toupees,
their burger-driven breath, their prune-sized
hearts—and then seem shocked when our lives
fit like barbed wire brassieres!

This is mostly what I've been trying to get at
with poetry, but maybe I overthink, maybe
I hyperbolize, maybe I pile on, maybe: maybe
I've lost sight of what people really want—

which is to cuddle the status quo
like a syphilitic teddy bear!

My mother used to say—before giving me
a good slap on the mouth—
You have gotten beside yourself, you
onion-headed little maniac   and she's right.

I *am* standing beside myself, this minute:
staring at myself staring back at myself,
asking, with a double dose of musty contempt,
"Why aren't you reading   my poems?!"

"PRAISE THE LORD!"

the poem shouts
from the corner,
a fresh *New Testament*
in its firm grip. Some people
look annoyed; some act
like the poem isn't
there. Because nothing

else has helped, because
Cruelty and Poverty
hold hands and hopscotch all over
the Earth's festering streets,
the poem now believes

in Jesus, the only son
God ever wanted, the only
hope for the fallen
flesh of which the poem
is regrettably made.

With so much
at stake and everything up
in the air, with Death's
fat belly pressed to its
grizzled cheek, the poem squeezes
the glory that only
the One Truth
provides. "Praise Him!"
What more

can a poem say?—
having spent most of its life
trying to say things *just so*, just
so people might reconsider
themselves and the apparent world.

The poem had once thought
that it could *itself* be
a way to refurbish the spirit:
retake the turf stolen
from the soul: a way to undo
the bad daily news
but the Great Shrug
had prevailed to spite
the words lined
on risers: each poem,

a small choir swaying—melody
after melody raised
from the dark—
renaming life, a testament
to the forgotten ecstasies.

"Hallelujah!" the poem shouts,
eyes closed, both hands
high above its head.

EXTRA BRIGHT BLUES VILLANELLE

Sometimes I guess I don't seem extra bright
Nobody tol' me *not* to stand behind that horse
Always thought the moon had its own light

I stay in the ring but keep losin the fights
Still got my gloves up, but my back's on the floor
Some days I guess I don't seem extra bright

Not tryin to *go gentle into that good night*
Meant to mean well, but there's always remorse
Don't it look like the moon makes its own light

If I had the choice I'd play your smile all night
But the brass teeth of Time keep chewin my door
I gotta believe the moon has its own life

Really don' know if I'll ever get right
Been charting the stars like a Martian off course
Sometimes they don't think that I seem extra bright

I think so much that my brain fits tight
They say I should act like a grown-up, of course
You ever believe the moon had its own light?

I'm climbin the walls of my day every night
Hard not to fear what the world's got in store
That's why I wish I could have extra sight

You ride with no hands when you ride with no bike
Where's Yoda at   when you're needin the Force

Sometimes I bet I don't seem extra bright
But I'm pretty damn sure the moon had its own light

SOMETHING LIKE WE DID

"Space Is the Place"
                —Sun Ra

You could tell they were surprised
that we still tried to build cities—
the way you and I might be amazed
that birds can build nests
without hands.

    They saw how we lived
    and made a sound like
    rain sifting a river.

        For a lot of us,
        knowing we were *not alone*
        brought relief from the headache
        that had lasted
        all our lives. Of course

some people were scared—the religious
held onto their books, claiming
this was all "make believe," even
when it was undeniable:
the sixty-one ships

    stacking light in the clouds—
    emerald green at dawn,
    lavender in late afternoon—
    the engines nearly quiet
    as if the sky were breathing.

        They walked something
        like we did, but the right foot
        stepped twice for each step
        of the left   so it appeared
        they were either testing the ground
        or considering a dance.

Their skin was dark
but transparent: their hearts,
like ours but visible

    and when the military began
    to mobilize, all the big weapons
    turned into barrels of wine and whatever
    we tried with knives or guns, we
    somehow ended up doing
    to ourselves   until it seemed
    insane   even to us.

        Each time one of them
        spoke   it was like a piano
        if Cecil Taylor were playing:
        voices bending the air
        the way chimney swifts
        swoop, half-turn, sling back.

But after awhile, when they
watched us, their lips shimmered

    and something *long ago*
    closed their eyes—

as if *we* were a memory
of who they once had been

    and they'd come to Earth
    to prove their existence

and mark the promise
of another world:

    someplace we might actually go
    if we could see inside ourselves

and trace what was there

ABOUT THE AUTHOR

Tim Seibles was born in Philadelphia in 1955. He has received fellow-ships from both the Provincetown Fine Arts Center and The National Endowment for the Arts. His collection *Fast Animal* was a finalist for the 2012 National Book Award and winner of the Theodore Roethke Memorial Prize for Poetry. His poems have appeared in numerous lit-erary journals, including *Ploughshares, Black Renaissance Noire, Rattle, Shenandoah, Callaloo, New Letters, Poetry,* and *The Massachusetts Review.* He spent a year as Poet in Residence at Bucknell University, and he recent-ly completed a two-year stint as Poet Laureate of Virginia.

A former faculty member of Old Dominion University's English Department and MFA in Creative Writing Program, Tim lives in Norfolk, Virginia, where he continues to teach for the Muse Community Writing Center. He has also led workshops for Cave Canem, The Writers Hotel, the Minnesota Northwoods Writers Conference, and the Palm Beach Poetry Festival.

A thoroughly engaged ambassador for poetry, he presents his work na-tionally and internationally at universities, high schools, cultural centers, and literary festivals. He has been a featured author in the Vancouver International Writers Festival in Vancouver Canada, in the Calabash Festival in Treasure Beach, Jamaica, and in the Poesia en Voz Alta Festival in Mexico City.

Tim Seibles is the author of eight previous books of poetry.

BOOKS FROM ETRUSCAN PRESS

Zarathustra Must Die | Dorian Alexander
The Disappearance of Seth | Kazim Ali
The Last Orgasm | Nin Andrews
Drift Ice | Jennifer Atkinson
Crow Man | Tom Bailey
Coronology | Claire Bateman
Topographies | Stephen Benz
What We Ask of Flesh | Remica L. Bingham
The Greatest Jewish-American Lover in Hungarian History |
     Michael Blumenthal
No Hurry | Michael Blumenthal
Choir of the Wells | Bruce Bond
Cinder | Bruce Bond
The Other Sky | Bruce Bond and Aron Wiesenfeld
Peal | Bruce Bond
Scar | Bruce Bond
Poems and Their Making: A Conversation | Moderated by Philip Brady
Crave: Sojourn of a Hungry Soul | Laurie Jean Cannady
Toucans in the Arctic | Scott Coffel
Sixteen | Auguste Corteau
Wattle & daub | Brian Coughlan
Body of a Dancer | Renée E. D'Aoust
Ill Angels | Dante Di Stefano
Aard-vark to Axolotl: Pictures From my Grandfather's Dictionary |
     Karen Donovan
*Trio: Planet Parable, Run: A Verse-History of Victoria Woodhull, and
     Endless Body* | Karen Donovan, Diane Raptosh, and Daneen Wardrop
Scything Grace | Sean Thomas Dougherty
Areas of Fog | Will Dowd
Romer | Robert Eastwood
Wait for God to Notice | Sari Fordham
Surrendering Oz | Bonnie Friedman
Nahoonkara | Peter Grandbois
Triptych: The Three-Legged World, In Time, and Orpheus & Echo |
     Peter Grandbois, James McCorkle, and Robert Miltner
The Candle: Poems of Our 20th Century Holocausts | William Heyen
The Confessions of Doc Williams & Other Poems | William Heyen
The Football Corporations | William Heyen
A Poetics of Hiroshima | William Heyen
September 11, 2001: American Writers Respond | Edited by William Heyen

ETRUSCAN PRESS IS PROUD OF SUPPORT RECEIVED FROM

Wilkes University

Youngstown State University

Ohio Arts Council

The Stephen & Jeryl Oristaglio Foundation

Community of Literary Magazines and Presses

[clmp]

National Endowment for the Arts

Drs. Barbara Brothers & Gratia Murphy Endowment

The Thendara Foundation

Founded in 2001 with a generous grant from the Oristaglio Foundation, Etruscan Press is a nonprofit cooperative of poets and writers working to produce and promote books that nurture the dialogue among genres, achieve a distinctive voice, and reshape the literary and cultural histories of which we are a part.

etruscan press
www.etruscanpress.org
Etruscan Press books may be ordered from

Consortium Book Sales and Distribution
800.283.3572
www.cbsd.com

Etruscan Press is a 501(c)(3) nonprofit organization.
Contributions to Etruscan Press are tax deductible
as allowed under applicable law.
For more information, a prospectus,
or to order one of our titles,
contact us at books@etruscanpress.org.